PRELIMINARY ASSESSMENT OF FISH ENTRAINMENT AT HYDROPOWER PROJECTS — A REPORT ON STUDIES AND PROTECTIVE MEASURES

1.0 INTRODUCTION

1.1 Need for this Report

The Federal Energy Regulatory Commission (FERC or Commission) considers protective measures for "identifiable environmental impacts" in the licenses it issues for nonfederal hydropower projects. The Electric Consumers Protection Act of 1986 requires FERC to balance power and nonpower values associated with hydroelectric development.

During consultation, resource agencies often request site-specific entrainment and turbine mortality studies to help quantify non-power values of affected fishery resources. Entrainment is the passage of organisms through water intakes. At hydroelectric projects, fish and other aquatic organisms frequently are drawn into turbine intakes where they may be injured or killed. Various life-stages of anadromous and resident fish may be entrained.

Since 1986 an increasing number of entrainment studies have been requested and conducted. Entrainment studies may not be needed, however, if existing data indicate that adverse impact is low or installing protective measures without studies is more cost-effective.

This report presents data from completed entrainment studies and draws inferences from these data, where possible. Licensees/applicants use many different approaches to study entrainment. These approaches often reflect differences in resource agency and/or consultant

guidance. Costs of studies also impact the level of study that a licensee/applicant provides. Because of the many different approaches to address entrainment issues, we recommend establishing a standard protocol for conducting entrainment studies. This document provides guidelines for building a standard protocol. However, assessment of the need for studies, as well as the actual study design, is based on a number of factors, including the expected level of impact and the cost of the studies.

Because resolution of entrainment issues is an ongoing iterative process, the database developed for this report can accommodate new data from future studies. This report addresses difficulties of data comparability.

1.2 Objectives

The objectives of this document, in descending priority, are as follows:

- summarize existing studies and analyze data to identify trends;

- assess the methods to use in future studies that address entrainment and protective measures; and

- evaluate the costs and effectiveness of commonly requested protective measures for reducing entrainment losses.

(this page intentionally left blank)

2.0 METHODS

2.1 Establishment of the Entrainment Review Team

Stone & Webster (SWEC) assembled an Entrainment Review Team (ERT) to provide guidance on the status and future of entrainment studies throughout the United States. Based on the location of sites where entrainment studies have been conducted, identified by FERC (Appendix 1), we invited representatives of the U.S. Fish and Wildlife Service (USFWS) regions and state fish and wildlife agencies where most of the entrainment studies have been conducted to participate on the ERT.

SWEC also contacted utility organizations, including the Edison Electric Institute (EEI), the Electric Power Research Institute (EPRI), the National Hydropower Association (NHA), and the Wisconsin-Michigan Hydro Users Group (HUG). Numerous utility representatives from these organizations responded to our invitation.

Two groups that commonly intervene in hydroelectric licensing proceedings, American Rivers and Trout Unlimited, were invited to participate, but failed to respond to the invitation.

SWEC organized two teleconferences (February 1 and 2, 1993) to explain the objectives of the project, solicit input from participants, and identify ERT members. Teleconference participants identified additional individuals to add to the mailing list to expedite the agency review process. As a result of the teleconference, we decided to include all individuals directly expressing an interest in participating or that were added to the project mailing list; this resulted in a large ERT (Table 2-1) but one that did not exclude any interest groups.

We asked ERT members to: 1) provide input on the content of the entrainment database, 2) review the draft database and provide comments on specific projects with which they were familiar, and 3) comment on the content of the draft interpretive report.

The U.S. Department of Energy (DOE) published a study comparing the cost-effectiveness of entrainment protective measures (Francfort et al., 1994). This DOE report should be used in conjunction with our report by those parties involved in evaluating the need for, or scoping entrainment studies at specific hydropower sites.

2.2 Derivation of the Entrainment Database

FERC staff compiled a list of all projects at which entrainment studies may have been performed. After an internal screening, 21 projects were eliminated from further consideration. We then evaluated the remaining 85 projects (Appendix 1) according to project objectives.

FERC provided SWEC with available entrainment study reports. When the study reports were not available from FERC, we contacted licensees, asked whether or not entrainment studies had been conducted at their project(s) and requested copies of the entrainment reports. Additional recently completed entrainment studies at Pixley, Upper and Lower projects were forwarded by FERC staff to SWEC as they were received. The ERT also identified pertinent entrainment studies that were not included in the Appendix 1 list.

TABLE 2-1
ENTRAINMENT REVIEW TEAM

Name	Entity Represented	Name	Entity Represented
Federal Agency Representatives			
Alex Hoar	USFWS (MA)	John Warner	USFWS (NH)
Ben Rizzo	USFWS (MA)	Hilary Zich	USFWS (PA)
Dave Bryson	USFWS (NY)	Rob Kelsey	USFWS (MD)
Gordon Russell	USFWS (ME)	Chris Clower	USFWS (WV)
Steve Gilbert	USFWS (SC)	Bob Krska	USFWS (MN)
Larry Oborny	USFWS (WI)	John Hamilton	USFWS (MI)
Don Sundeen	USFWS (OR)	Rich Greenwood	USFWS (MI)
Jennifer Hill	FERC (DC)	Jim Lynch	FERC (DC)
John Ramer	FERC (DC)		
State Agency Representatives			
Mark Woythal	NY Dept. Env. Cons.	Gary Whelan	MI DNR
Ed Radle	NY Dept. Env. Cons.	Walt Houghton	MI DNR
Jim Rawson	WV DNR	Tom Thuemler	WI DNR
Leroy Young	PA Fish & Boat Com.	Karl Sheidegger	WI DNR
Wayne Davis	KY Dept. Fish & Wildlife	Will Reid	Idaho Fish & Game Dept.
Gerrit Jobsis	SC Wildlife and Marine Resources Dept.		
Utility Representatives			
Bob Richter	Central Maine Power Co. (EEI)	Linda Hinseth	Wisconsin Power & Light Co. (EEI)
Keith Corneau	Adirondack Hydro Dev. Corp. (EEI)	Dave Michaud	Wisconsin Power & Light Co. (HUG)
John Sulaway	New York Power Authority (EEI)	Tony Maio	EEI
Tom Tatham	New York Power Authority (EEI)	Lowell Neudahl	Minnesota Power (EEI)
Kevin McGrath	New York Power Authority (EEI)	Alan Gaulke	Am. Elect. Power Service Corp. (EEI)
Gary Schoonmacker	Niagara Mohawk Power Corp. (EEI)	Bruce Eddy	Pacific Corp. (EEI)
Dave Fingada	Rochester Gas & Electric (EEI)	Brian McGurty	So. Calif. Edison Co. (EEI)
John Crutchfield	Carolina Power & Light Co. (EEI)	Tom Jareb	Pacific Gas & Electric Co. (EEI)
George Galleher	Duke Power Co. (EEI)	Jack Mattice	Electric Power Research Institute
Charles Sullivan	Electric Power Research Institute		
Additional Experts			
Glenn Cada	Oak Ridge National Lab.		

We evaluated all available study reports for inclusion in the database. In general, we included studies if the sampling effort was sufficient to ensure a reasonable level of confidence in the entrainment estimate derived from the data. We did not include sites that were geographically isolated (e.g., Mokelumne and Elwha) or involved pumped storage (e.g., Big Creek No. 8 & 2A) because data from these sites were not considered to be comparable to data from other sites due to species and operational differences. Appendix 1 describes the rationale for not including a report in the database.

The parameters for the database were established in the original task description and supplemented by SWEC and the ERT. Tables in the database contain variables that can be quantitatively analyzed. Variables that require qualitative comparisons are included in the narrative part.

Data extracted from the entrainment reports were supplemented by information contained in license application documents or other sources such as U.S. Geological Survey Water Yearbooks. We converted entrainment information for each site to a standard unit of measure: number of fish per hour. We also included the total annual number of fish entrained at each site. Appendix 2 contains a detailed description of each data field in the tabular portion of the database.

We sent draft databases, with copies of calculation sheets showing the sources of information, to the project licensee/applicant and members of the ERT. We asked licensees/applicants to verify the accuracy of the database entries, review the appropriateness of assumptions made to convert entrainment data to the

standardized format, and provide data for any blank fields. We asked ERT members to comment on the adequacy of the studies and to review the assumptions made in deriving the data. In some cases, both the licensee and an ERT member provided blank field information. When the information conflicted, we assumed the licensee's information was the most accurate. The narrative portion of the database contains comments on each study.

2.3 Development of the Entrainment Protective Measure Cost and Effectiveness Questionnaire

SWEC developed a questionnaire to collect information on the costs of conducting entrainment studies and implementing protective measures and the effectiveness of installed protective measures. Although we did not duplicate previous work such as that performed by DOE (Sale et al., 1991) some overlap between this study and previous studies is unavoidable.

We asked the Idaho National Engineering Laboratory (INEL), which previously solicited information by questionnaire on the cost of entrainment and turbine mortality studies and protective measures for the DOE study, to review our questionnaire. We incorporated INEL's and FERC's suggestions into our final questionnaire (Figure 2-1).

SWEC mailed the questionnaire to licensees/applicants of the 157 projects scheduled to be relicensed by the end of 1993. We selected these licensees because many of them had conducted entrainment studies as recommended by resource agencies during the consultation process. We were able to assemble entrainment

Figure 2-1

COST QUESTIONNAIRE: ENTRAINMENT ABUNDANCE STUDIES,
TURBINE MORTALITY STUDIES AND PROTECTIVE MEASURES

RETURN TO:
Douglas Hjorth
Stone & Webster Env.
Services
PROJECT NAME_____ 245 Summer St.
Boston, MA 02210
FERC NO._____

ENTRAINMENT ABUNDANCE AND TURBINE MORTALITY STUDIES

COSTS OF ENTRAINMENT ABUNDANCE STUDIES (separate hydroacoustic
and netting costs, if possible) _____
_____

COSTS OF TURBINE MORTALITY STUDIES (indicate basic sampling mode,
e.g., tailrace netting)_____

TIME SPAN OF ENTRAINMENT STUDIES _____

ENTRAINMENT PROTECTIVE MEASURES (installed or costs estimated)

YEAR PROTECTIVE MEASURE INSTALLED_____, OR YEAR
COSTS ESTIMATED _____

ENTRAINMENT PROTECTIVE MEASURES (e.g., travelling screens,
slotted screens, fish bypass systems, angled bar racks, inclined
screens, barrier nets, spill flows, attractant and repellant
measures)_____
_____
_____
_____

DESCRIPTION OF PROTECTIVE MEASURES (attach additional sheets if
needed)_____
_____
_____
_____
_____
_____
_____

IS PROTECTIVE MEASURE INTENDED ONLY TO EXCLUDE FISH FROM TURBINE
PASSAGE OR ALSO TO FACILITATE PASSAGE? (indicate which) _____
_____

MAXIMUM FLOW CAPACITY (CFS) OF UNIT(S) WITH PROTECTIVE DEVICES
_____

Figure 2-1 (Continued)

DESIGN APPROACH VELOCITY (FPS) PERPENDICULAR TO SCREEN (if applicable)_____

COSTS OF ENGINEERING DESIGN FOR ENTRAINMENT PROTECTIVE MEASURES

_____

YEAR(S) IN WHICH ENGINEERING DESIGN COSTS INCURRED_____

COSTS OF CONSTRUCTING ENTRAINMENT PROTECTIVE MEASURES _____

_____

YEAR(S) IN WHICH CONSTRUCTION COSTS INCURRED_____

ANNUAL OPERATION AND MAINTENANCE COSTS (indicate the year that such costs were derived,also) _____

ANNUAL COSTS OF LOST GENERATION ATTRIBUTABLE TO PROTECTIVE DEVICE (include the basis for the costs)_____

_____

ANNUAL COSTS OF FOLLOW-UP ENTRAINMENT MONITORING STUDIES AND ASSOCIATED REPORTING REQUIREMENTS _____

YEAR(S) IN WHICH ENTRAINMENT MONITORING STUDIES WERE CONDUCTED OR ARE PROPOSED _____

EFFECTIVENESS OF THE PROTECTIVE MEASURE AND BASIS FOR DETERMINING EFFECTIVENESS (cite reports, if possible) _____

_____
_____
_____
_____
_____
_____
_____
_____
_____
_____
_____
_____
_____

LIST ANY OTHER COST ELEMENTS ASSOCIATED WITH THE INSTALLED PROTECTIVE MEASURE _____

_____
_____
_____

NAME, TITLE AND TELEPHONE NUMBER OF PERSON FILLING OUT QUESTIONNAIRE_____

COMMENTS:

and turbine mortality costs for studies conducted during the last several years. Costs for potentially recommended protective measures also were likely to have been developed by many applicants where entrainment mortality was considered to be high. The DOE study (Sale et al., 1991) presented costs for many studies and protective measures implemented between 1980 and 1990. We expected the responses to our questionnaire to reflect most recent costs available and to be useful in providing guidance for implementing future studies and/or protective measures.

Distributing the questionnaire only to those licensees with expiring licenses did not provide a substantial amount of new information on the effectiveness of installed entrainment protective measures, since most projects scheduled to be relicensed would not normally install protective measures until after the license was issued. DOE conducted a detailed study on the cost-effectiveness of many conventional entrainment protective measures, however, as a follow-up to its 1991 report. The DOE study (Francfort et al., 1994) obviates the need to generate a similar analysis as part of our study.

2.4 Analytical Approach

2.4.1 Qualitative Trend Analysis

Certain variables in the database are not amenable to statistical analysis. For example, nearly all intakes of the studied hydropower projects are oriented perpendicular to the flow of the river; only three intakes are oriented parallel to the direction of flow. Consequently, the trend analysis for this variable consists of a qualitative assessment of entrainment patterns at these three sites and how they differ from sites with perpendicular oriented intakes.

Because of variable sampling and reporting conventions, it is difficult to make quantitative intersite comparisons. The size composition of entrained fish is a good example of such variability. The minimum size detected by hydroacoustic methods varies between sites and often at the same site for different plant operating conditions. The minimum size captured in nets also varies across studies. In addition, the size of fish collected by nets is sometimes reported as a species-specific length range, by size intervals of the total number of fish collected, or as tables of individual measurements of each fish collected.

Generalizations about the size of entrained fish at different sites are possible and are included in this report. More rigorous statistical treatment of these data is not possible, however, without standardized reporting of length-frequency data. Additional variables that were evaluated for trends qualitatively, for reasons similar to those described above, include the number of units sampled, the proportion of total flow sampled, the study method used (netting or hydroacoustics), and the relative entrainment rates between units.

The specific type of analyses conducted depended on the availability of pertinent information in the database and individual study reports. When possible, we prepared a comparative table and evaluated the data for the presence of consistent trends for our qualitative assessment. If a trend was evident, we reviewed the database for factors that were common to those sites exhibiting similar trends. If an entrainment study at a specific site provides useful insight into a factor that could influence entrainment rates at other sites, we describe the salient findings of the study.

2.4.2 Quantitative Trend Analysis

We conducted quantitative analysis of entrainment data in two parts: an exploratory regression analysis, which included an evaluation of the effect of individual, high leverage data points; and a supplemental analyses, which included these high leverage data points. We examined potential relationships between physical site parameters and the total entrainment rate (for all species and sizes combined) in both sets of analyses. We did not perform species- and size-specific statistical analyses because of the limited number of studies that provided estimates of total entrainment rates by species and size collected in a comparable manner. We did group and analyze sites as a block, however, if they had similar species assemblages of entrained fish. We performed all analyses for two entrainment variables: the average annual entrainment rate (fish per hour) and the flow-adjusted rate (fish per hour per 1,000 cfs of plant capacity).

We conducted the exploratory regression analysis using Version 2 of JMP (SAS, 1989); the "Fit Y by X" platform in JMP fit both linear and quadratic lines for each variable. We examined plots of each regression to identify individual high leverage data points that cause or mask a significant association. The high leverage points were typically from sites with exceptionally high rates of entrainment or where the value of the particular site variable was substantially different from all other sites. We examined the effect of any outlier data points by removing them from the data set and evaluating changes in the significance of the regressions.

We performed each exploratory regression on the following data sets:

1) all available data;
2) all available data excluding sites dominated by clupeids;
3) only sites employing full-flow tailrace nets (also excluding sites dominated by clupeids); and
4) individual watersheds where data were available from two or more sites.

Our supplemental analyses included a correlation analysis, a principal components analysis, and a regression analysis using species assemblages as a covariate.

We performed the correlation analysis using the JMP (SAS, 1989) analysis platform "Y's by Y's" to calculate the Pearson product moment correlation and scatterplot matrices. We used the JMP analysis platform "Spin" to conduct the principal components analysis. We used the JMP analysis platform "Select Model" to perform the regression analysis using species assemblage as a covariate. In this last analysis, we grouped sites into assemblage categories based on the predominant groups of species represented in entrainment samples.

2.4.3 Rationale for Selecting Representative Species

Comparisons of entrainment for all species may mask trends associated with individual species. Because a comparison of entrainment rates for all species included in the database was impractical, however, we selected representative species to evaluate entrainment rates of important sportfish and forage fish in addition to the total entrainment rate. We did not group representative species for this analysis (i.e., centrarchids, cyprinids, percids) because each species has unique habitat requirements and behavioral characteristics. We evaluated monthly entrainment rates of these representative species to identify trends over time.

We selected smallmouth bass and walleye as representative sportfish. Both species were entrained at many sites in Michigan and Wisconsin, where the majority of studies in the database were conducted. Sufficient data were available to indicate whether or not there were trends in entrainment rates.

We selected black crappie and yellow perch as representative panfish. Both species are often sought by anglers and are an important recreational fishery resource. They also are both common at sites in the midwest and the southeast, which gives a broader geographic analysis of entrainment rates than is possible for smallmouth bass or walleye.

SWEC selected white sucker and two species of clupeids as representative forage fish. White suckers were collected often enough in entrainment samples in Michigan and Wisconsin to enable potential trends to be identified. This species has a wide geographical range, and, if trends were apparent at the sites in the database, the pattern may be appropriate to explore at sites not included in the database.

Clupeids are an abundant forage base in certain parts of the country and, in many cases, habitat preference and behavioral patterns among species are similar. The two species of clupeids with sufficient entrainment data in the database are gizzard shad and threadfin shad. Entrainment trends of these two species may provide insight into entrainment trends of other clupeids throughout the country.

3.0 RESULTS

3.1 Geographical Distribution of Sites

All of the studies included in the entrainment database were conducted at sites east of the Mississippi River (Figure 3-1). Hydroelectric projects west of the Mississippi (in California, Oregon, Washington, and Idaho) often install screens with bypass facilities (especially at sites with anadromous fish), which minimizes the need to conduct entrainment studies (personal communication, letter from Gerry Jackson, Acting Regional Director, USFWS, to Douglas Hjorth, SWEC, dated April 16, 1993). Most sites (24 of 45) are within the Great Lakes drainage, nine sites each are within the Upper Mississippi and Mid-Atlantic Coastal drainages, and four sites are within the Upper Ohio River drainage.

The greatest number of projects in the database (18) are in Michigan, followed by Wisconsin (12), and South Carolina (6) (Figure 3-2). Resource agencies in these states often recommend site-specific entrainment studies.

3.2 Database Analysis

3.2.1 General Findings

The database includes results from entrainment studies at 45 sites. Most studies were conducted at hydropower projects with an electrical capacity of less than 5.0 MW (Figure 3-3), but electrical capacity ranges from 0.56 MW (Tower) to 102 MW (Hawks Nest). Hydraulic capacities range from 360 cfs (Tower) to 35,598 cfs (Greenup Lock and Dam); the capacity at most sites is less than 3,000 cfs (Figure 3-4).

Entrainment Study Methods

The database's most striking characteristic is the variability in methodologies. Hydroacoustic studies, which varied both in the number of units sampled and in the proportion of the flow sampled at each unit, often were designed to be supplemented by netting studies. In one case (Crowley) hydroacoustic estimates supplemented tailrace netting collections. Frequently, both netting and hydroacoustic techniques were used, and the most appropriate estimate was determined at the end of the study. Although approaches differed, all study plans were developed in consultation with, and in most cases approved by, state and federal resource agencies.

Netting entrainment was estimated by using partial-flow tailrace nets, partial-flow turbine gallery nets, partial-flow forebay nets, full-flow tailrace nets, and combinations of partial and full-flow nets that varied either spatially or over time. The number of units sampled by nets ranged from 10 percent to 100 percent of the units. Netting effort was extremely variable, ranging from a low of 8 hours per month at Lock and Dam #2 to a high of 720 hours per month at Youghiogheny. Sampling efforts varied between sites, and in some cases, at the same site (e.g., monthly sampling efforts at Millville ranged from 24 to 589 hours).

At some sites there were no net efficiency studies, most often because net collections were designed to provide species and size composition data to support hydroacoustic sampling. Various approaches were used for net efficiency studies. At some sites, net efficiency was

Numbers next to project locations are
FERC project numbers.

Figure 3-1

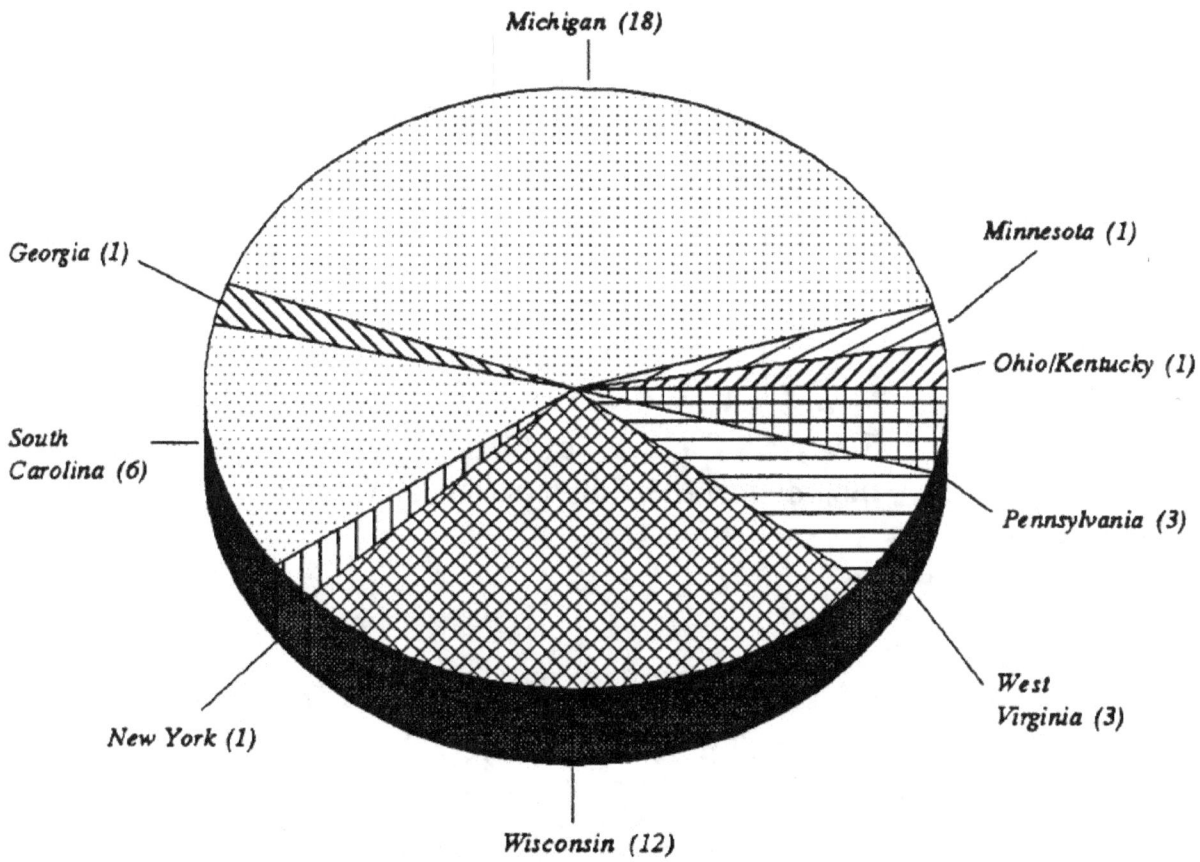

Figure 3-2
Distribution of Sites by State
Included in the Entrainment Database

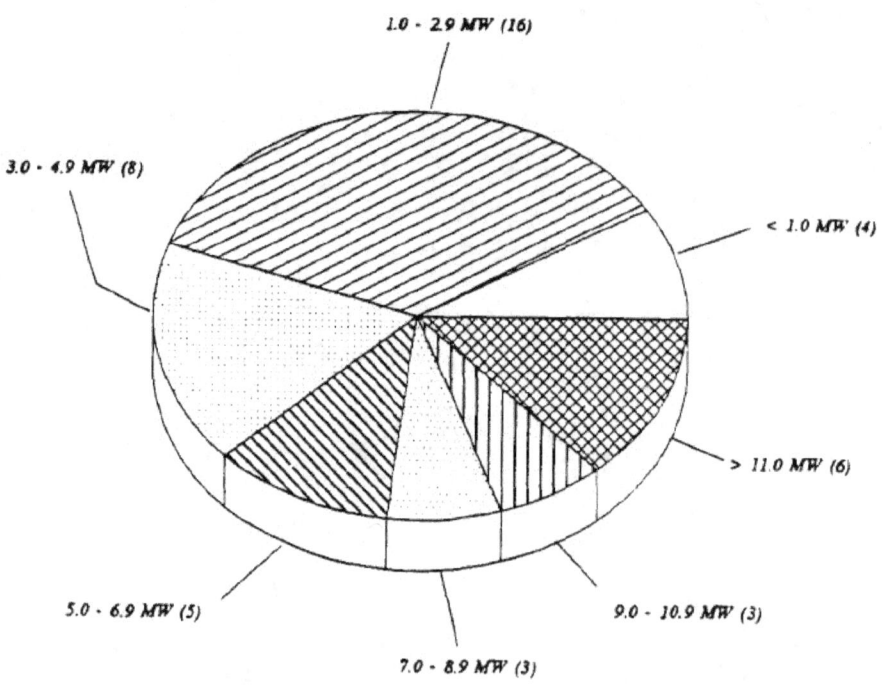

Figure 3-3
Electrical Capacity of Sites
Included in the Entrainment Database

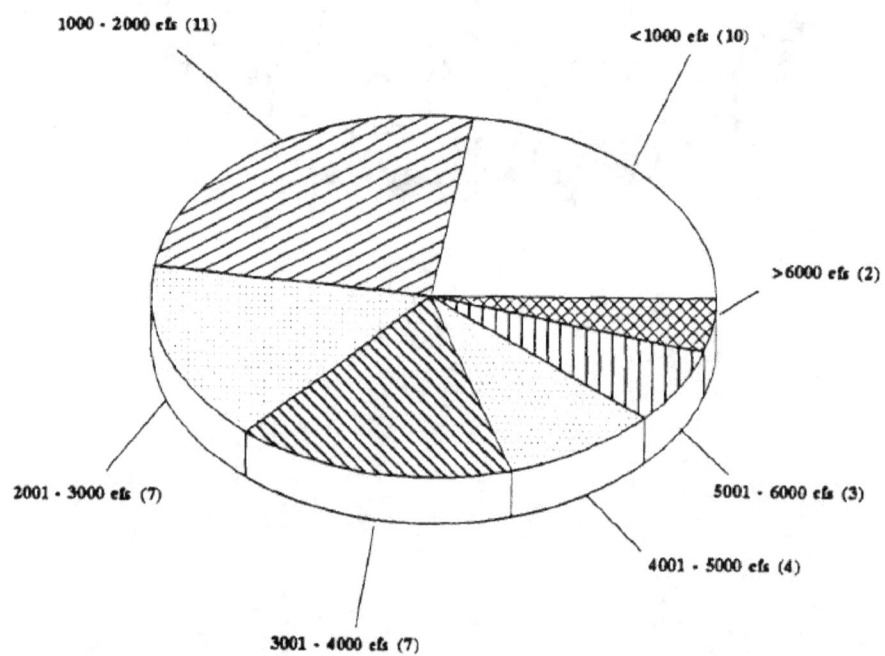

Figure 3-4
Hydraulic Capacity of Sites
Included in the Entrainment Database

determined by releasing fish in front of the turbines and recovering them in tailrace nets. Sometimes test fish were released directly into the mouth of the net. Other sites combined these two approaches (e.g., Thornapple). At some sites, both live and dead fish were released; other sites used either. Size and species of test fish, frequency of efficiency tests, and the statistical treatment of efficiency test results varied.

Statistical derivation of entrainment estimates also varied substantially. Studies at some sites never reported an annual entrainment estimate, and insufficient information is available to derive it. At sites in South Carolina, the entrainment rates derived during the study year were applied to typical plant operating conditions, which in some cases were different from the conditions during sampling (both in terms of volume passing through the plant and amount of time that each unit operated). Elsewhere, the entrainment estimate represented only the year sampled.

Entrainment rates derived from netting studies are based on either the number of fish per unit of time or unit of volume sampled. Rates are then applied to the amount of time that each unit operates during a year or the volume of water passing through each unit during a year to derive average annual entrainment estimates. At some sites with multiple units, the entrainment rate was assumed to be the same at sampled and unsampled units. Other studies attempted to account for differences in entrainment rates at different units. Entrainment estimates at some sites (e.g., Buchanan and Constantine) used geometric means of data to account for non-normal distribution of the sampled population. Most studies, however, used arithmatic means. (FERC practice has been to accept entrainment estimates derived from arithmatic means.)

An important factor when considering comparability of data between sites is the minimum size of fish counted. For example, the minimum size hydroacoustic target sampled at Hawks Nest was 3 inches. It would be difficult to compare these data to data from Centralia, where, according to netting results, most entrained fish were less than 1.5 inches.

Often non-entrained fish are collected in tailrace netting, especially with partial-flow nets. These fish add uncertainty to the estimated size distribution of fish collected during studies. Representativeness of independently derived species and size composition is a critical assumption in adjusting the fish counts derived from hydroacoustic studies.

Comparing the size distribution of fish collected at the Centralia and Hawks Nest projects illustrates the potential significance of small fish in an annual entrainment estimate. Both sites used nets with 0.75-inch bar mesh, yet the entrainment rates of small individuals were vastly different. This difference is probably due to different species assemblages (see Section 3.2.5 for more information on species assemblage influences).

Although adjusting entrainment estimates in the database to include only fish over a certain size would make estimates more comparable, it would be difficult to select the appropriate size cut-off point. Many entrainment estimates derived from netting data include some fish less than 1.5 inches; other estimates exclude fish less than 3.0 inches (e.g., the hydroacoustic target limit at Hawks Nest). The minimum size of fish included in entrainment estimates may even vary at the same site, which is especially true with hydroacoustic methods because the minimum detection size varies under different sampling conditions. For example at Loud, the minimum size fish detected during optimum conditions was 2.0 to 2.5 inches; under high flow conditions, the minimum size detected was 4 to 5 inches.

Another difficulty in adjusting entrainment estimates is that fish size information is not reported in a uniform manner. Some reports list the lengths of all fish collected (e.g., Buzzard's Roost for non-threadfin shad and Station 26). Others present size distributions by species or for all species combined (using a variety of size intervals) (e.g., Hawks Nest). Others report only the length range of entrained fish.

Even if the entrainment estimates were adjusted to include only larger sized fish, this would effectively eliminate the majority of entrained fish. To make size comparisons, future size distribution reporting/recording requirements for fish collected in entrainment studies must be standardized (see Section 4.5).

Variability of Results

Given the range of study methods, plant characteristics, and fish populations represented, study results are quite diverse. Dam No. 4 had the lowest estimated annual entrainment rate (0.6 fish/hour) and Buzzard's Roost had the highest (2,492 fish/hour) (Table 3-1).

On rivers with more than one entrainment study documented, the downstream-most project tended to have higher annual entrainment rates (e.g., the Black, St. Joseph, Escanaba, Wisconsin, Broad, and Saluda rivers) than upstream projects. Hydropower projects are normally sized to accommodate available river flow, and downstream projects generally pass more water (and potentially more fish) than upstream projects.

To account for variable plant hydraulic capacities, however, we calculated the flow-adjusted entrainment rate (annual entrainment rate divided by the plant hydraulic capacity in thousands of cfs) for each project. This adjustment eliminated the trend for the St. Joseph, Broad, and Saluda rivers. The trend remains strong at the remaining three rivers, however, which may be related to species-specific habitat preferences. For example, the annual entrainment rate on the Wisconsin River is driven by the abundance of young channel catfish (most of which were collected in July at all three sites). This species comprised only 5.1 percent of the entrainment estimate at the most upstream plant, Rothschild, whereas it comprised 32.7 and 75.3, percent, respectively, of the total entrainment estimates at the Wisconsin River Division and Centralia projects. Habitat for catfish would be expected to improve in the lower gradient reaches (generally downstream) of most rivers, which may partially explain the trend on the Wisconsin River.

On the Menominee River, there is an inverse relationship in annual entrainment rates; more fish (mostly common shiner and bluegill) were entrained at the most upstream site than at the downstream site (mostly rock bass and bluegill). No upstream-downstream trends were evident on the Au Sable or Flambeau rivers. On rivers with obvious trends, however, the number of data points (two or three) is too low to predict any relationships based on river mile or location.

State	River	River Mile	Site	Annual Entrainment Rate Fish/Hour	Fish/Hour/kcfs
Michigan	Au Sable	73	Mio	13.7	5.1
		38	Alcona	10.3	3.2
		33	Loud	18.6	7.1
		29	Five Channels	48.7	16.2
		22	Cooke	25.4	7.0
		12	Foote	17.7	4.4
			Mean	**22.4**	**7.2**
	Muskegon	89	Rogers	6.4	2.7
		58	Hardy	3.0	0.7
		47	Croton	25.1	6.8
			Mean	**11.5**	**3.4**
	Grand	-	Moores Park	9.8	8.2
	Black	-	Tower	3.4	9.4
		-	Kleber	7.2	18.0
			Mean	**5.3**	**13.7**
	St. Josephs	103	Constantine	5.4	3.1
		33	Buchanan	8.0	2.1
			Mean	**6.7**	**2.6**
	Sturgeon	44	Prickett	13.2	20.6
	Escanaba	3	Escanaba Dam 3	2.5	2.0
		1	Escanaba Dam 1	5.2	4.4
			Mean	**3.8**	**3.2**
	Huron	-	French Landing	181.9	227.4
Minnesota	Mississippi	26	Lock & Dam #2	--	--
Wisconsin	Menominee	55	White Rapids	16.5	3.2
		4	Park Mill	5.3	2.1
			Mean	**10.9**	**2.7**
	Brule	2	Brule	4.8	3.5
	Flambeau	-	Upper	6.4	8.9
		-	Lower	11.8	12.7
		-	Pixley	5.6	8.3
		-	Crowley	7.6	5.1
		8	Thornapple	7.0	5.0
			Mean	**7.7**	**8.0**

TABLE 3-1 (page 1 of 2)
ANNUAL ENTRAINMENT RATES BY RIVER AND STATE

TABLE 3-1 (page 2 of 2)
ANNUAL ENTRAINMENT RATES BY RIVER AND STATE

State	River	River Mile	Site	Annual Entrainment Rate	
				Fish/Hour	Fish/Hour/kcfs
Wisconsin (cont.)	Wisconsin	258	Rothschild	24.3	7.4
		220	Wis. River Division	80.6	15.7
		199	Centralia	95.2	26.2
			Mean	**66.7**	**16.4**
	Wolf	-	Shawano	4.6	5.5
Georgia	Savannah	220	King Mill	15.8	--
South Carolina	Broad	-	Gaston Shoals	17.9	6.7
		-	99 Islands	18.6	4.1
			Mean	**18.2**	**5.4**
	Saluda	-	Saluda	8.3	10.4
		103	Hollidays Bridge	12.8	8.0
		60	Buzzards Roost	2492.2	623.0
			Mean	**837.8**	**213.8**
	Rocky	13	Abbeville	12.4	31.8
West Virginia	New	8	Hawks Nest	5.5	0.1
	Potomac	188	Dam #4	0.6	0.3
	Shenandoah	6	Millville	3.5	1.6
Ohio/ Kentucky	Ohio	341	Greenup Lock & Dam	--	--
Pennsylvania	Beaver	6	Beaver Falls	34.6	7.8
	Youghiogheny	73	Youghiogheny	212.4	132.7
New York	Genessee	7	Station 26	30.8	17.1

Note: When more than one site is located on a river, the site at the most upstream location is listed first. Double dashes (--) indicate that the rate could not be estimated.

Many studies report variable or episodic entrainment over the course of the study year (e.g., Prickett, Brule, and Beaver Falls). Episodic entrainment events are usually more easily detected by hydroacoustic techniques because they generally sample a larger proportion of the total available time than possible using net techniques. The size and species composition of entrainment episodes, however, can best be characterized by netting. At the Youghiogheny entrainment study, the most comprehensive netting survey in the database, full-flow tailrace netting at both discharge bays was conducted continuously for a full year. Of the estimated annual entrainment of 1,578,452 alewives, 45.3 percent were estimated to have been entrained during a 1-week period in early January. A relatively high entrainment rate of adult walleyes also was documented at the same time. One hypothesis to explain this extremely episodic entrainment is that the low water temperature caused alewives to become moribund and less able to escape the intake approach velocity. Walleye apparently followed the alewives into the vicinity of the turbine units, making them more vulnerable to entrainment.

Diel Trends

There were few consistent diel patterns (daily variances) of entrainment at the sites included in the database. Total entrainment rates were similar during the day and night at 10 of the 21 sites that addressed this issue. There were qualitative trends for certain species (such as ictalurids that generally were more commonly entrained during the night at Gaston Shoals), but some trends were only present during scattered months with no apparent pattern (e.g., Ninety-nine Islands and Saluda).

Entrainment rates were generally higher at night at most (eight of nine) of the sites exhibiting a diel trend for total species entrainment rate. At one of these sites, Buzzard's Roost, the entrainment rate of all species except the dominant species was more common at night, whereas threadfin shad were more common during the day. In contrast, at Youghiogheny, the alewife entrainment rate was six times greater at night. The intake at the Youghiogheny Project is located at a depth of over 30 feet, but the Buzzard's Roost intake is relatively close to the surface (within 3 feet).

The divergent trends in diel entrainment rates probably relates to behavioral characteristics of clupeids, which are plankton feeders. Because plankton is more prevalent in the upper water column during the day, they would be more susceptible to entrainment at a surface-oriented intake during the day. Only one site, French Landing, reported consistently higher entrainment rates during the day, and entrainment at this site is dominated by black crappie and bluegill.

Variation of Entrainment Between Years

Most entrainment studies to date have been conducted over a 12-month period. The assumption with this approach is that the year sampled is representative of typical entrainment rates at that site.

Entrainment studies at Millville and Dam No. 4, which were conducted over multiple years, provide data for assessing year to year variability of entrainment rates. Data from Millville are the most useful for this comparison because samples were collected during at least part of four different years, plant conditions were relatively stable, and the annual entrainment rate is more typical of the rates at other projects than Dam No. 4. Although there are some data available from two years for Dam No. 4, between the two years, a third unit was added.

The database presents monthly entrainment rates for both Millville and Dam No. 4 for the single unit that was sampled. These rates are, therefore, valid for making between-year comparisons. Between-year comparisons for total annual entrainment rates at Dam No. 4, however, are not valid because the total entrainment rate for the second year includes extrapolated entrainment for the added unit.

The relative abundance of species collected at Millville remained markedly similar from 1986 to 1991 in spite of the varying level of sampling effort (Table 3-2). Centrarchids and channel catfish were dominant species during all 4 years. On occasion, species that were usually infrequently collected were dominant in collections during a specific year (e.g., shorthead redhorse and American eel). In general, the four species most often entrained were relatively consistent.

There also was relative consistency in abundance of species collected between years at Dam No. 4. Centrarchids and channel catfish comprised the top seven most frequently entrained species at this site in 1986. Other than some displacement by greenside darter and American eel, the species composition was similar during the 2 years sampled.

Even at these two sites with similar species composition from year to year, there is enough variability in peak entrainment timing to underscore the unpredictable nature of entrainment. At both sites any 1 year of data would yield a reasonable approximation of the species most likely to

be entrained, but periods of peak entrainment and entrainment rates varied between years.

The total monthly entrainment rates at Millville during the four study years show some similarities for peak entrainment rate (Figure 3-5). In general, data indicate that the highest entrainment rates occur from April to June and drop precipitously in July or August. Considering that the dominant species are centrarchids, this drop corresponds with the period when most adults would be in near-shore areas guarding their nests and, therefore, would be less likely to be entrained. Peak entrainment rates again occurred in September and/or October in 1989 and 1991, presumably reflecting the entrainment of juvenile fish. A fall peak was not evident in 1986.

If the annual entrainment rate for one year is assumed to be representative of other years, then shifts in monthly occurrence of peak entrainment rate are not important as long as the magnitude of the peak entrainment periods is comparable. Entrainment rates ranged from 3.7 to 5.1 fish/hour during April, 2.1 to 3.8 fish/hour in May, and 3.7 to 6.2 fish/hour in June, indicating reasonable agreement in the entrainment rate. Greater variability in entrainment abundance was evident in the fall, however, with rates ranging from 0.1 fish/hour during 1986, when no fall peak was evident, to 3.5 fish/hour during 1991.

Although the entrainment study plan for most projects called for only one year of data collection, in some cases there was overlap in the months sampled. This allowed monthly entrainment rates to be estimated for two separate years (Table 3-3) providing an additional measure of year to year variability. Comparative monthly rates (see Table 3-3) indicate that at some sites

	1986 (5 months)*		1989 (4 months)*		1990 (9 months)*		1991 (12 months)*	

TABLE 3-2
RELATIVE ABUNDANCE OF ENTRAINED FISH COLLECTED AT MILLVILLE FROM 1986 TO 1991

	1986 (5 months)*		1989 (4 months)*		1990 (9 months)*		1991 (12 months)*	
	% Comp	Rank	% Comp	Rank	% Comp	Rank	% Comp	Rank
Bluegill	21.4	1	31.4	1	16.4	3	26.6	2
Redbreast Sunfish	20.1	2	11.6	3	27.5	1	38.5	1
Channel Catfish	17.1	3	25.0	2	13.1	4	2.8	6
Smallmouth Bass	9.1	4	3.5	6	2.8	7	7.8	4
Common Carp	7.9	5	2.3	8	1.1	8	0.3	13
Yellow Bullhead	5.6	6	1.7	11	0.4	12	0.6	8
Pumpkinseed	5.0	7	3.5	6	3.0	6	2.4	7
Largemouth Bass	2.5	8	1.2	12	0.4	12	0.3	13
Shorthead Redhorse	1.9	9	2.3	8	27.5	1	0.5	10
Rock Bass	1.8	10	0.6	15	3.4	5	5.1	5
Golden Redhorse	1.7	11	NC	NC	0.1	23	NC	NC
Margined Madtom	1.3	12	1.2	12	<0.1	30	<0.1	23
Green Sunfish	1.1	13	7.5	4	0.2	18	0.2	15
White Crappie	1.0	14	NC	NC	NC	NC	NC	NC
UID Sunfish	0.2	20	4.0	5	0.3	14	0.1	17
American Eel	0.4	17	2.3	8	0.1	23	11.8	3
Black Crappie	NC	NC	1.2	12	0.2	18	0.1	17
Number of Fish Collected	1995		199		3520		5321	

* Number of Months Sampled

NC = Not Collected

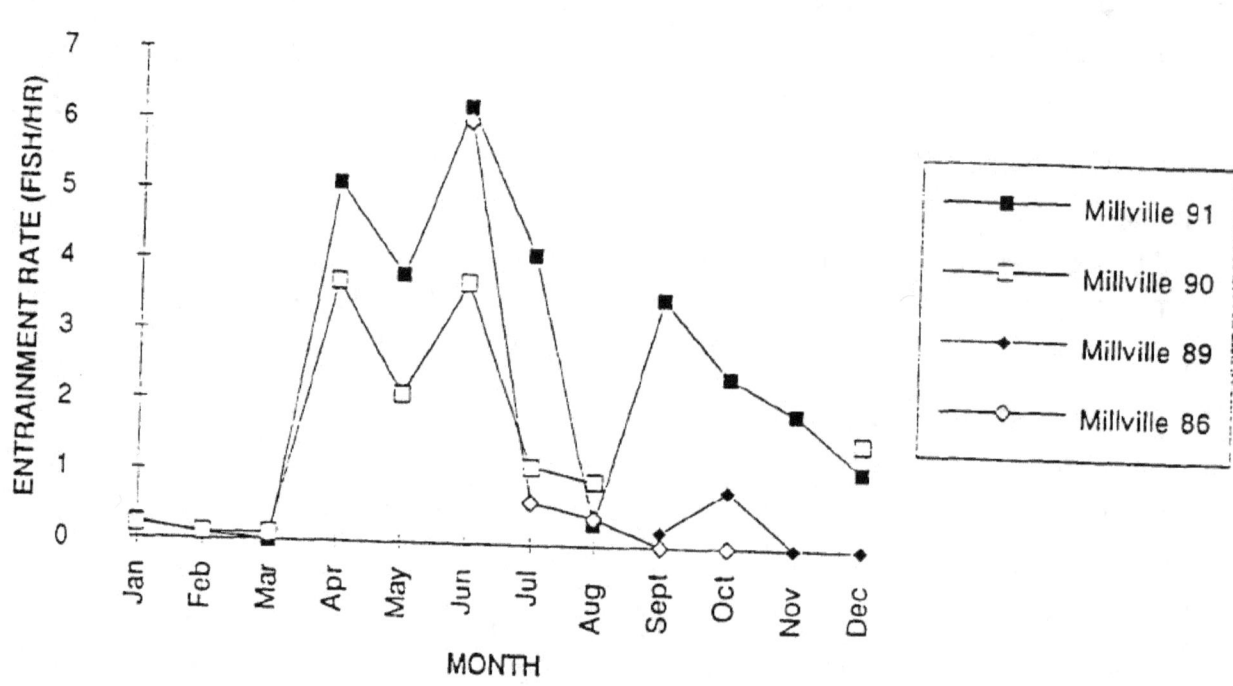

Figure 3-5
Millville Monthly Fish Entrainment for
1986, 1989, 1990 and 1991

Site	Year	April	May	June	July	August	Septmbr.	Octbr.
TABLE 3-3 **YEAR-TO-YEAR VARIABILITY IN TOTAL MONTHLY ENTRAINMENT** **RATES AT SITES INCLUDED IN THE DATABASE** **(Fish per Hour)**								
Moores Park	1	--	--	--	--	--	13.80 (69 F)	--
	2	--	--	--	--	--	19.50 (75-76 F)	--
Tower	1	11.35 (67 F)	--	--	--	--	--	--
	2	9.16 (54-56 F)	--	--	--	--	--	--
Kleber	1	111.38 (65 F)	--	--	--	--	--	--
	2	0.70 (40-45 F)	--	--	--	--	--	--
French Landing	1	--	--	--	774.40	--	--	--
	2	--	--	--	121.40	--	--	--
Station 26	1	--	--	8.80	24.60	115.40	55.90	128.70
	2	--	--	6.80	23.20	38.50	37.30	61.50
Dam No. 4	1	1.88	1.61	0.94	0.30	0.13	0.65	0.16
	2	0.50	0.50	0.30	0.80	0.30	0.60	0.40

Note: All entrainment rates except those for Station 26 derived from netting data. Water temperature at the time samples were collected (when available) shown in parenthesis. Refer to Figure 3-5 for comparison of monthly rates at Millville.

monthly entrainment rates were similar; at others, entrainment rates were two to more than 100 times greater during the same month but different years. In some cases, this variation may be caused by temporal shifts in peak entrainment events related to environmental factors such as water temperature which influences fish movements (e.g., an unusually cold spring may postpone increased centrarchid activity from April to May). Substantially cooler water temperatures may have caused the dramatically different entrainment rates during April at Kleber (Table 3-3). At Tower and Moores Park slightly higher entrainment rates were associated with higher water temperatures. Monthly water temperatures at Millville were generally comparable for the 3 years for which data were available. Year to year variability may reflect the episodic nature of many entrainment events and whether these episodes coincided with the entrainment sampling effort.

In some cases entrainment rates are higher when water temperatures are higher. Sampling during a warmer-than-average year may provide a conservative entrainment estimate. One obvious exception to this is when extremely low temperatures result in high entrainment rates of moribund fish. When entrainment sampling results indicate episodic entrainment due to unusual temperature conditions, available long-term temperature records can be consulted. Such records could show the expected recurrence rates of such temperatures and any resultant episodic entrainment.

Entrainment of Rare Species

According to entrainment reports, collection of rare species of fish is infrequent. State-listed threatened species were only collected at two sites in the database: Buchanan and Rothschild. A single river redhorse, listed by Michigan as threatened, was collected at Buchanan. A black buffalo and greater redhorse, both listed as threatened by Wisconsin, were collected at Rothschild. Because both individuals collected at Rothschild were too wide to fit through the 1.4-inch trashracks, however, they probably are the result of tailrace intrusion. We found no accounts of entrained federally-listed threatened or endangered species in the database reports.

3.2.2 Comparison of Different Sampling Techniques

Studies included in the database used three basic methods for sampling: 1) partial-flow netting, 2) full-flow netting, and 3) hydroacoustics. Partial-flow netting was most frequently used in the tailrace. Where this was impractical, partial-flow net sampling was conducted in front of the turbines. Full-flow netting most often was used in the tailrace of one or more units, and hydroacoustics normally sampled fish in front of the turbines.

Partial-Flow Netting

Partial-flow netting provides data on species and size composition when full-flow tailrace netting is not possible because of physical limitations, high through-turbine discharges (e.g., Lock and Dam No. 2 and Greenup Lock and Dam), or when hydroacoustic techniques are the primary method for estimating entrainment.

Partial-flow tailrace netting often samples resident fish in the tailrace that are not entrained, however, which causes overestimates of entrainment. Intrusion can introduce substantial error into the estimated size distribution, because large fish are common in tailraces. If the net is positioned in relatively low velocity water, fish may also swim out of the net after being collected. Sampling a zone in front of the turbines where all fish are not committed to entrainment can result in under- or overestimation of entrainment rates. Any net sampling behind the trashracks, however, can cause serious damage to the turbines if a net breaks loose.

Full-Flow Netting

Full-flow tailrace netting is normally preferable to partial-flow netting because of the larger flow volume sampled and because tailrace intrusion of fish is limited. Some tailrace intrusion still may occur with use of full-flow tailrace netting, most likely through gaps between the net and the powerhouse.

Netting Techniques Compared

Entrainment rates as measured by partial and full-flow tailrace netting were estimated at the Rogers Project. Partial-flow tailrace sampling was used at the discharge of units 3 and 4 (estimated aerial coverage: 8.5 percent) year-round. Partial-flow netting also was used at the discharge of Units 1 and 2 from January, March, and early April; after mid-April full-flow tailrace netting was used. The database segregates data for Rogers by unit and presents the combined entrainment estimate for the entire plant to make it easy to compare the two collection techniques.

The licensee's consultant conducted an analysis of variance (ANOVA) to compare the collection densities and length-frequency distributions of fish collected on four separate sampling dates in September and October (when entrainment rates were relatively high and not considered to be biased). Results indicated no significant difference between the two sampling methods. The licensee did not, however, conduct an ANOVA to assess sampling

method differences during the spring. Tailrace intrusion was suspected at other sites sampled by partial-flow tailrace netting during the spring due to localized spawning migrations of walleye and white sucker.

Annual entrainment estimates for Units 1 and 2 (25,059) and Units 3 and 4 (30,816) were similar. Monthly entrainment rates for all species and sizes combined showed somewhat greater variability, ranging from 0.00 to 6.95 fish/hour at Units 1 and 2 and 0.2 to 11.7 fish/hour for Units 3 and 4 during April to December. Entrainment rates for June, August, September, and December were comparable but dissimilar (differences of 2 to 40 fold with the partial-flow estimates always higher) for April, May, July, and October.

Species-specific monthly entrainment rates also were usually similar. More shorthead redhorse and chinook salmon were collected in full-flow nets (Units 1 and 2), however, than in partial-flow nets (Units 3 and 4). Most shorthead redhorse and chinook salmon were relatively large (9 to 17 inches) and may be able to sense the presence of the partial-flow net and have sufficient burst swimming speed to avoid capture. Further investigations would be necessary to confirm this hypothesis, but the Rogers data suggests the potential to underestimate entrainment rates of certain species with partial-flow netting. There was no apparent source of bias from unit location.

The Rogers data indicate that partial-flow tailrace net results are similar to those of full-flow nets. The average monthly entrainment rate (all species) estimated by partial-flow nets was either comparable or higher than for full-flow nets. According to these data, partial-flow nets give a conservative estimate of the entrainment rate. For some species (e.g., shorthead redhorse and chinook salmon), however, entrainment estimates may not be conservative. Partial-flow nets should be positioned in high velocity locales to minimize possible tailrace intrusion and fish swimming out of the net after capture.

Hydroacoustics

Hydroacoustic techniques have the advantage of providing potentially less costly continuous sampling at many different locations. Fish also can be counted without incurring injury or death, which sometimes results from other collection techniques. A disadvantage of hydroacoustic techniques is that with high noise, it may be difficult or impossible to obtain accurate hydroacoustic counts of all but the largest fish. In addition, low intake velocities often preclude the use of this technique because fish detected may not be committed to entrainment. Some net collections to confirm the species and size distribution must be used unless these parameters are clearly evident (e.g., juvenile blueback herring at Mohawk River sites).

Entrainment rate estimates obtained by hydroacoustics and netting are usually within three-fold of each other and, in some cases, quite similar. Table 3-4 compares total entrainment estimates obtained using both methods at the same site. Estimates obtained by partial-flow tailrace netting were lower than the hydroacoustic estimate in six of seven cases. Because netting at these seven sites was primarily intended to provide species and size distribution information in conjunction with hydroacoustic estimates, however, the net collection effort was relatively low (24 to 48 hours per month) and the mean number of fish collected per year at these seven sites was only 301 (range: 60 to 851). The entrainment rate estimates are not as precise

as estimates based on larger numbers of collected fish. Estimates obtained by full-flow netting (nine comparisons) or partial-flow turbine gallery netting (one comparison) were similar in three cases and higher (more conservative) than the corresponding hydroacoustic estimates in seven of ten cases. Generally, over 1,000 fish were used to derive full-flow and partial-flow turbine gallery netting annual entrainment rate estimates. These data indicate that sampling with full-flow tailrace nets and possibly partial-flow turbine gallery nets gives conservative estimates of entrainment rates.

Table 3-4 shows the variability in the minimum detectable size (1 to 5 inches) of hydroacoustic targets between sites and, in some instances, at the same site. The table also illustrates the variability in mesh sizes used in netting studies (0.25- to 1-inch bar). Estimating the size effectively sampled by net is difficult because it is influenced both by mesh size and flow characteristics. The importance of establishing standardized acceptable minimum sized fish for entrainment rate estimates is apparent if you consider that more than 50 percent of the annual entrainment estimate at Centralia comprises fish that are less than 1.5 inches long.

3.2.3 Relative Entrainment Between Units and Influence of Intake Configuration on Entrainment Rates

Entrainment rates may differ between units because of temporal and spatial factors. The most common temporal factor is the amount of time that a unit is operated. Units that operate more frequently than others tend to entrain more fish. For example, 62 percent of the entrained fish at

	Hydroacoustics			Netting		
Site	Minimum Size Detected (inches) Under Following Conditions		Annual Rate[2] (fish/hr)	Annual Rate[2] (fish/hr)	Type of Net[3]	Net Bar Size (inches)
	Optimum[1]	High Discharge				
Alcona	2-3	--	10.27	5.26	PFTR	1
Cooke	1.75	--	25.39	6.30	PFTR	1
Loud	2-2.5	4-5	18.55	1.87	PFTR	1
Mio	1.75	3-4	13.74	4.34	PFTR	1
Five Channels	2-3	--	48.73	2.50	PFTR	1
Croton	1.75	3	25.09	17.00	PFTR	1
Hardy	1.75	3	2.96	12.40	PFTR	1
Park Mill	-54dB[4]	--	5.31	5.56	PFTG	0.75
Moores Park	2	--	9.80	10.65	FFTR	0.25
Tower	2	--	3.40	3.08	FFTR	0.25
Kleber	2	--	7.20	17.34	FFTR	0.25
White Rapids	1	--	5.92	16.50	FFTR	0.75
Brule	1	--	2.89	4.80	FFTR	0.75
Crowley	2	--	7.90	7.60	FFTR	0.25
Shawano	--	--	4.60	4.90	FFTR	0.25
99 Islands	4	--	18.60[5]	27.20	FFTR	0.75
Gaston Shoals	4	--	10.50	17.90	FFTR	0.75

(1)   Optimum = low discharge, minimal extraneous sound.
(2)   Underlined annual rate is considered to be the best estimate by the applicant and/or resource agency. In cases where the hydroacoustic estimate was considered most representative, the primary purpose of the netting samples was to provide species composition and length frequency information to apply to the hydroacoustic data.
(3)   PFTR = Partial flow tailrace netting; PFTG = Partial flow turbine galley netting; FFTR = Full flow tailrace netting.
(4)   Acoustic size presented in decibels; actual size not presented.
(5)   Annual entrainment estimate adjusted for proportion of fish collected in nets that were less than four inches long.

White Rapids were detected at Unit 1, which operated twice as much as the other two units. Similarly, 68 percent of entrained fish at Brule were detected at Unit 2, which operated more frequently than the other units. At Youghiogheny, 73.3 percent of all fish were collected at Unit 1. This unit was operating during a 1-week entrainment episode in early January when nearly half of the annual alewife entrainment occurred.

Another temporal factor influencing entrainment rates between units is volume per unit of time. The south unit at Moores Park entrained twice as many fish as the north unit because wicket gate problems reduced the flow through the north unit. At Rothschild, only 21 percent of the fish were collected at one of the two units sampled. The unit with higher entrainment had greater flow and higher approach velocities.

Spatial factors also influence differences in entrainment rates between units and, in some cases, within the forebay of the same unit. Some plants have a forebay configuration in which one unit is much closer to the shoreline than other units. Unit-specific entrainment studies at such sites show that entrainment abundance is generally higher at near-shore intakes. Hydroacoustic studies at Shawano illustrate this trend. Of the targets, 55 percent were detected at the shoreside intake, 33 percent at the center intake, and 12 percent at the riverside intake. The same trend was documented at Greenup Lock and Dam, where more fish were collected at the near-shore intake during all three seasons that were sampled. This pattern was attributed to the tendency for fish to follow the shoreline of rivers. At both Shawano and Greenup Lock and Dam there are no power canals or other structures that would tend to evenly distribute fish across the intakes. Differences between units also were evident

at Park Mill, where more than twice as many fish were collected in the net closest to an area of relatively still water within the forebay area.

Several additional entrainment studies illustrate the effects of intake location on entrainment. The intake of Escanaba Dam 1 is in a relatively shallow portion of the impoundment. Most of the entrained fish were sunfish, which most frequently are found in shallow-water habitats. The peak entrainment rate noted in June was attributed to increased sunfish activity as they moved to their preferred spawning and residence areas, and the October peak was attributed to entrainment of young-of-the-year centrarchids. Considerably fewer sunfish were entrained at Escanaba Dam 3, where the Dam 3 powerhouse is located near the center of the dam, away from the shallow, littoral zone favored by sunfish.

The proximity of shallow, near-shore habitat also appeared to influence entrainment at the Kings Mill Project on the Augusta Canal. A bed of aquatic plants is located immediately upstream of the shoreline intake of this project. The October peak in the entrainment rate correlated with the senescence of aquatic plants; those fish that normally rely on these plants for cover would be more wide-ranging when the cover is gone and thus more vulnerable to entrainment. One proposed protective measure at this site was to reconfigure the intake by constructing a wall on the upstream side to withdraw water from the deeper part of the canal rather than in proximity to shallow water nursery areas.

The influence of the proximity of the intake to the shoreline also is evident at the Beaver Falls Project. The entrainment catch at this site was strongly dominated by gizzard shad (85.6 percent of the entrained population), the same species that dominated the catch at Greenup Lock and Dam where there was a positive relationship between proximity of the unit to the shoreline and the entrainment catch.

The intake to the Beaver Falls Project is flush with the shoreline and separated from the dam spillway by a pier. Full-flow tailrace netting was used to sample one of the two intakes at this project. Only one unit was operated during much of the entrainment study, but a study was conducted to determine the validity of applying the entrainment rate at the sampled unit (determined volumetrically) to the unsampled unit. Two day-time trials and one night-time trial were conducted. Sampling was performed for equal periods of time with one and two unit operation.

Study results showed an 87 to 88 percent decrease in entrained fish density at the sampled unit during two-unit operation. Forebay turbulence and noise during two-unit operation may have deterred schooling young gizzard shad from entering the intake. The study concluded that sampling entrainment at only one unit probably overestimated the total plant entrainment rate. The annual entrainment estimate from the sampled unit was presented as a conservative estimate of the total plant entrainment (i.e., the volume of water passing through the unsampled turbine was not considered in deriving the annual entrainment estimate for the facility). It is debatable whether or not this conclusion was justified by the available data. It is evident, however, that the entrainment rate at the Beaver Falls Project with two units operating is not double the entrainment rate of a single unit operating.

We compared entrainment rates at sites with forebay intakes to those with power canal intakes. Eight sites in the database have a power canal intake. Annual entrainment rates at seven of these projects (Constantine, Buchanan, Prickett, Park Mill, Upper, Hollidays Bridge, and Millville) range from 3.50 to 13.24 fish/hour (Table 3-1) and are comparable to those with forebay intake configurations. The eighth site is Centralia, where the annual entrainment rate of 95.20 fish/hour is higher than the rate at most plants with forebay intakes, but comparable to the 80.60 fish/hour at the plant upstream of Centralia which has a forebay intake, Wisconsin River Division. Study results show that the entrainment rate at projects with power canals is likely to be of similar magnitude to those projects with forebays.

The intakes to three sites in the database are oriented parallel to the prevailing flow. One site, the King Mill Project, illustrates that proximity to shoreline habitat may influence entrainment rate. The other two sites, Buchanan and Station 26, illustrate other influences on entrainment rates.

The intake at Buchanan is on a power canal that diverts water from the St. Joseph River. All 10 units are located on one side of the canal, which dead-ends adjacent to Unit 10. Entrainment sampling was conducted at Units 4, 7, and 9. The dominant species collected were chinook salmon and rainbow trout smolts. Both species were stocked 30 miles upstream of the project in March, April, and May, and were collected at Buchanan during April, May, and June. Most chinook salmon and rainbow trout, as well as resident species, were consistently collected at Unit 9, which is the unit closest to the dead-end of the canal. No chinook salmon or rainbow trout were collected at Unit 4. The total number of fish collected at each unit was:

- Unit 4- 181;
- Unit 7- 700; and
- Unit 9- 2218.

There is distinct pattern of increased entrainment rate with increased proximity to the end of the power canal.

The Rock Island Dam powerhouse on the Columbia River (Raemhild et al., 1984), which has an intake configuration similar to that at Buchanan, showed a similar pattern. Ten turbine units were monitored during the period of peak downstream migration of salmon and steelhead (rainbow trout). The unit closest to the end of the power canal entrained 35 percent of the total catch; the seven units closest to the upstream end of the canal each entrained no more than 5 percent of the total catch.

The intake to Station 26 (in New York) is parallel to the main flow of the Genesee River. It is immediately upstream of a dam and directly across from a non-power related intake structure that also is oriented parallel to the river flow. Both power and non-power intakes run along the shoreline. Entrainment at this site is dominated by clupeids (an estimated 83.4 percent of entrained fish), most of which are gizzard shad. There was a shift in passage from the upstream end of the intake structure in June to the downstream end in September that was documented by hydroacoustic techniques. Based on netting collections, the spring entrained fish were spottail shiner and the fall entrained fish were gizzard shad. The indicated shift over time from upstream to downstream entrainment, therefore, is probably due to changing species composition rather than to changing behavioral patterns of the same species. Overall, the middle intake bays exhibited the lowest entrainment rate.

Another important aspect of the Station 26 entrainment study is the avenue of downstream fish movement. Passage through the powerhouse, through a non-power intake across the river from the powerhouse intake, and over the dam spillway was monitored hydroacoustically. Analysis indicated that most fish passed over the spillway. During the 9 months of concurrent monitoring of the power and non-power intakes, however, the entrainment rates (fish/hour) through each intake were comparable. This is especially noteworthy because the flow through the non-power intake averaged 75 cfs, and the flow through the power intake averaged 1,594 cfs. This is consistent with the trend at the Beaver Falls Project that entrainment rates at sites dominated by clupeids are not necessarily related to water volume through the intake.

3.2.4 Horizontal and Vertical Distribution Within Units

Sometimes the location of hydroacoustic transducers allows assessment of distribution trends within individual forebays. At Croton, Tower, and Unit 1 of Mio there was no horizontal distribution pattern of entrainment. At Alcona, however, 81 percent of the hydroacoustic targets were detected along the right or left side of the intake and only 19 percent in the center of the forebay. The same pattern occurred at Unit 2 of Mio with only 19 percent passing through the center of the forebay. The horizontal distribution assessment at Foote showed that two-thirds of the fish were detected along the forebay side closest to the shoreline of the two units sampled.

Reported vertical distribution patterns, determined hydroacoustically, were inconsistent. There was no pattern at Croton, Kleber, or Station 26, and fish tended to be slightly deeper during the day at Park Mill. Entrained fish were more frequently detected in the top of the water column at Tower, Lock and Dam No. 2, Crowley, and Ninety-nine Islands, and fish were most often detected at mid-depth at Moores Park. At Saluda and Hollidays Bridge, there was no vertical trend for most of the period sampled, but during November to January, more fish were detected at the top of the intake at Saluda, and during November and December, more fish were detected at mid-depth at Hollidays Bridge.

3.2.5 Quantitative Trend Analysis

We conducted quantitative analyses of entrainment data in two parts. First, we performed an exploratory regression analysis to identify statistically significant trends between entrainment rates and single physical variables that were subjectively determined to have potential significance. This exploratory analysis also examined the effects of individual, high-leverage observations in the data set that explained most of the statistically significant associations between the entrainment rate variables and other physical parameters. The second part of the analysis included a correlation analysis, a principal components analysis, and a regression analysis on a larger set of variables. Our second analysis did not evaluate the effect of high-leverage observations on the significance of the associations. In our second set of regression analyses we used a species assemblage covariate that was not used in the exploratory regression analysis.

Exploratory Regression Analysis

We conducted the exploratory analysis to identify statistically significant trends or associations between entrainment rates and individual physical characteristics of the hydro projects, waterbodies, or their reservoirs. We used the "Fit Y by X" platform in JMP to fit linear and quadratic lines for each variable.

The database includes a fairly large range of values for the independent physical site parameters evaluated. The distribution of observations within each range tends to be clustered except for a few observations. These non-clustered observations can exert disproportionate leverage on the significance and degree of association between variables. We used a series of regression analyses with a single variable to identify associations between the variables. We did not classify as significant those associations established by the value of a high-leverage observation. We used a 0.05 probability level as the significance criterion. We also visually reviewed the scatter plots for weak trends that could not be identified by calculation of a 0.05 probability level.

Site parameter variables include: reservoir surface size, reservoir length, total reservoir storage, plant flow, reservoir flush rate, depth of intake, trashrack spacing, and average velocity. We tested each variable against the average annual entrainment rate (fish/hour) and the flow-adjusted entrainment rate ([total fish/hour]/kcfs). Where entrainment rates had not been extrapolated to all units, we substituted the capacity of the units represented by the entrainment rate estimate (the entrainment flow) for the plant capacity for this calculation (see column H5 of the database in Appendix 3).

When SWEC constructed the database, it seemed that if there were clupeid species at a site, there were higher entrainment rates. Each analyses described above, however, also was conducted using a modified database excluding sites where the entrainment rate was dominated by clupeids (King Mill, Buzzard's Roost, Hawks Nest, Greenup Lock & Dam, Beaver Falls, Youghiogheny, and Station 26). Because some resource agencies question the acceptability of entrainment rate estimates derived by hydroacoustic and partial netting techniques, we also performed additional analyses using only full-flow tailrace netting at sites not dominated by clupeids.

To account for watershed variations, we conducted separate analyses for three basins with more than four sampled sites: the Au Sable River Basin (Alcona, Foote, Cooke, Loud, Mio, and Five Channels), located in Michigan; the Flambeau River Basin (Thornapple, Crowley, Upper, Lower, and Pixley), located in Wisconsin; and Broad River Basin (99 Islands, Gaston Shoals, Saluda, Hollidays Bridge, and Buzzard's Roost), located in South Carolina.

We did not include two sites (Lock and Dam #2 and Greenup Lock and Dam) in the 45-site database in our statistical analyses or summaries because they did not offer reliable entrainment rate estimates. In the 43 studies that were available for analysis, the values for one or more variables (other than entrainment rate) sometimes were incomplete. The number of observations available for analysis is set by the number of non-missing values for the specific variable. We could not always conduct watershed analyses because of missing values. For some variables, such as usable reservoir storage, a meaningful analysis could not be conducted because of limited available data.

We summarize results of our exploratory data analyses in the following section. Details of this statistical analysis are presented in Appendix 4.

Reservoir Size

Neither the linear nor the quadratic analyses yielded a significant positive association between reservoir size (as measured by surface acres) and flow-adjusted or average entrainment rate when two high-leverage sites were dropped from the analysis. The watershed-based analysis also showed no significant relationships between entrainment and impoundment size when high-leverage sites were dropped from the analysis. The trends in the occurrence of high-leverage sites are typically repeated for each variable analyzed. Sites such as Buzzard's Roost, which have high entrainment rates and larger reservoir size, flush rate, plant flow, total reservoir storage, and depth, show high-leverage observations for each variable.

The 24 exploratory analyses relating entrainment rates to reservoir size showed no consistent, significant trends in the database for this variable.

Reservoir Length

The 24 exploratory analyses relating entrainment rates to reservoir length showed no significant associations.

Total Reservoir Storage

The 24 exploratory analyses relating entrainment rates to total storage showed no significant associations when one or two large reservoir sites with high entrainment such as Youghiogheny and Buzzard's Roost were dropped from the analysis.

Plant Flow

The analysis for all data showed no significant trends in either flow-adjusted or average entrainment rates and plant flow with or without the Hawk's Nest, Buzzard's Roost, and Prickett sites (all high-leverage for this variable). When the high-leverage Buzzard's Roost site was dropped from the watershed analysis, the two analyses for the remaining four Broad River sites showed an interesting trend in plant flow: for the flow-adjusted entrainment rate, there was a significant negative association with plant flow, while the average entrainment rate was not significant but the scatterplot showed a positive association with plant flow. An association was observed for the Broad River sites after one high-leverage data point was removed; however, this association was based on only four remaining observations.

There are two possible inferences for the Broad River sites: 1) more fish/hour are entrained at the higher flow sites, and 2) the numbers of fish/hour adjusted for flow rate decrease in proportion to flow. The first is intuitive, perhaps expected at any hydro project, and it is surprising that the other watershed analyses for this variable are not similar, although pulses of large numbers of young-of-the-year fish may mask this trend. The second inference is less intuitive and may be an artifact of other physical conditions associated with plant flow. There are no obvious reasons for these trends. Some "significant" trends may occur by chance alone.

Through-plant Reservoir Flush Rate

Many of these analyses produced significant positive associations with flush rate. In most cases, however, significance disappeared when a single observation was eliminated.

Depth of Intake Submergence

None of the initial analyses on this variable yielded significant associations. Even when the Buzzard's Roost and Youghiogheny sites (which have greater entrainment rates than the other sites) are dropped from the analysis, there were no significant trends.

Trashrack Spacing

The analyses show no consistent associations between entrainment rate and the single variable of trashrack spacing, perhaps because the majority of entrained fish are small and easily pass through typical trashrack spacings at sites where entrainment studies have been conducted.

Average Intake Velocity

There were no significant trends between entrainment rate and average velocity.

Conclusions of Exploratory Analyses

Our analyses of variables for which meaningful amounts of information are available indicate no consistent statistically significant trends for total number of entrained fish. Analyses for individual species could be undertaken, but the species-specific data sets contain even fewer observations than those used for total species. The species-specific data appear to be at least as variable, if not more so than the data for total entrainment rates. Much of the variability probably relates to sampling and reporting methods that vary among studies.

Supplemental Analyses

Correlation Analysis

Correlation, which is a measure of association between variables, can vary from -1 to +1 in value. A correlation value of 1 between two variables indicates a close and positive association between the values of the two variables. A correlation of 0 indicates no association and an independence in the values of the two variables. A correlation value of -1 between two variables indicates a close and negative association between the values of the two variables.

We compared the correlation of 11 physical site parameters with both the average entrainment rate and the flow-adjusted entrainment rate (average entrainment per 1,000 cfs plant capacity). We used the JMP (SAS, 1989) analysis platform "Y's by Y's" to calculate the Pearson product moment correlation and scatterplot matrices. We created a separate table of correlations for each entrainment rate. Each table shows correlation coefficients for each combination of the 11 variables. To accompany each table, we also created a scatter plot matrix for each pair of observations. We provide details of this analysis in Appendix 5.

Our analysis showed high positive correlation of the flow-adjusted entrainment rate with usable storage (0.9964), reservoir width (0.9962), and reservoir flush rate (0.9584). The cross correlation (correlation among the independent, non-entrainment rate variables) of these three variables also was very high. These high correlations were expected, as the previous regression analyses showed that one or two high-leverage observations lead to significant associations. Those same high-leverage observations are contained in the data set used for the correlation, principal components, and additional regression analyses.

The average entrainment rate showed a high, positive correlation with average velocity (0.9959) and trashrack spacing (0.9559). The average entrainment rate was also negatively correlated with reservoir length (-0.9480). Trashrack spacing was cross correlated with average velocity. Reservoir length showed a high negative cross correlation with average velocity and trashrack spacing. Other non-target variables with high positive cross correlation included: reservoir size and total storage; reservoir size and reservoir (through-plant) flush rate; and, entrainment flow and plant flow.

Some correlations are expected based on typical engineering practices used at the time the plants were designed and on the physical conditions of the site. For example, reservoirs with large usable storage are generally also relatively wide. Also, a project designed with a relatively high average water velocity probably has large trashrack spacing.

Correlation of the flow-adjusted entrainment rate with usable storage and reservoir width indicates that the rate of entrainment per unit flow increases with the usable storage and reservoir width. The correlation of the flow-adjusted entrainment rate and reservoir flush rate may be because both variables are functions of flow rate.

Average entrainment rate is cross correlated with average velocity and trashrack spacing. Sites with high average velocity generally have larger trashrack spacing. The average entrainment rate is negatively correlated with reservoir length, which indicates that shorter reservoirs in the data set were associated with higher entrainment rates.

The high correlations observed for entrainment rates with various physical variables and the cross correlation among the physical variables do not, however, indicate a predictive trend in entrainment variables. Correlation only explains associations between variables in a data set. Although this analysis did not review the effects of the high-leverage observations identified during the exploratory analysis, these high-leverage observations probably have many observed correlations.

Principal Components Analysis

Principal components analysis develops linear combinations of variables that explain the greatest amount of variation. The coefficients of these linear combinations, which are called eigenvectors, are calculated from the correlation matrix. There are as many linear combinations (or principal components) calculated as there are variables of interest. Each linear combination accounts for a particular amount of data variability. When the data are highly correlated and a large number of variables of interest are included in the calculation, a few principal components account for nearly all the variability in the data set. The individual values of the eigenvectors cannot be used to judge the correlation of individual pairs of variables.

We conducted the principal components analysis with 11 physical site parameters and one of the two entrainment rate variables; the analysis was conducted twice. We used the JMP (SAS, 1989) analysis platform "Spin" with the principal components option to calculate the tables of

principal components. We present details of this analysis in Appendix 3.

All the variability in the data set can be explained by three principal components. This result is expected because the correlation analysis showed close correlation between many independent variables. The principal components table for the flow-adjusted entrainment rate and the same 11 physical variables shows a very similar distribution (or accounting) of the variability in the first three principal components. Although these three principal components accounted for all the variability in the data set, they cannot be used to predict entrainment rates at other sites.

Regression Analysis

As discussed previously, the exploratory analyses of average entrainment and flow-adjusted entrainment rate for eight univariate analyses yielded no strong, consistent trends.

We further explored these interrelationships with some additional approaches. We reviewed the species composition data and segregated the 42 sites with this type of data into 6 species assemblages. The assemblages are based on the species that accounted for 10 percent or more of the species composition entrained at each site. Some species assemblages were indicative of particular habitat types (these habitat types are in parentheses).

1. Clupeid dominated sites - Station 26, Youghiogheny, Beaver Falls, Greenup, Buzzard's Roost, Lock & Dam #2, King Mill, and Hawks Nest. We could not distinguish all sites where most entrainment occurred during the winter, because some sites did not have species composition or

entrainment abundance sampling in the winter season. This may be important because in the winter, moribund fish may inflate entrainment, as suspected at Buzzard's Roost and Youghiogheny.

2. Ictalurid, white sucker, darter, American eel (benthic species assemblage) - Wisconsin River Division, Centralia, 99 Islands, Dam 4, Foote, Tower, and Gaston Shoals.

3. Walleye, yellow perch, black crappie, smallmouth bass (offshore species assemblage) - Cooke, Rogers, Mio, Hardy, Kleber, Escanaba 1, Brule, Crowley, Abbeville, French Landing, and Rothschild.

4. Rock bass (near-shore, hard substrate species assemblage) - Alcona, Loud, Five Channels, and Park Mill.

5. Lepomis, cyprinids (near-shore soft/sandy substrate species assemblage) - Croton, Moores Park, Prickett, Shawano, Saluda, Hollidays Bridge, Millville, Constantine, White Rapids, and Thornapple.

6. Salmonid dominated sites - Buchanan and Escanaba 3.

Because assemblage 6 is not represented by enough sites to be a separate covariate for the analysis, for our analysis we merged it with assemblage 5 (the remaining species at these sites and the habitat is most similar to that of assemblage 5). Also, although the Upper, Lower and Pixley sites did not report species composition data, these sites probably would be most like Crowley, and we included them in assemblage 3.

We used these assemblages as blocks or covariates in a reanalysis of our previous exploratory data analysis. This analysis does not drop outlier sites but adjusts the means of the groupings as covariates. The output of the analysis yields an average entrainment and flow-adjusted entrainment rate for each assemblage and a test to quantify a regression against the 11 physical variables.

We used the JMP (SAS, 1989) analysis platform "Select Model" to develop a regression analysis of one of the two dependent entrainment rates (average entrainment or flow-adjusted entrainment rates) against the assemblage code and one additional independent variable among the 11 physical variables used for both the correlation and principal components analysis. We also developed a larger model for both entrainment rate variables using the two or three independent variables that were most highly correlated with the average entrainment and flow-adjusted entrainment rates. We evaluated the value of these higher order models compared to the simple covariate models. We present details of this analysis in Appendix 5.

For the flow-adjusted entrainment rate, we observed statistically significant responses for average river flow, reservoir size, total storage, usable storage, and trashrack spacing. There also was a marginally significant response for reservoir flush rate. The statistical significance of some of these regression tests is at least partly attributable to outliers in the data set. The multiple variable model is not justified to explain and summarize the available data over the use of the simple single variate models with the assemblage covariate.

For the total average entrainment rate, we observed statistically significant responses for reservoir size, total storage, usable storage, and trashrack spacing. Again, the statistical significance of some of these regression tests is partly attributable to high-leverage observations in the data set.

The multiple variable regression with average velocity, trashrack spacing, and reservoir length was not statistically significant for any of the individual variables in this combination of independent regressors, even though the correlation analysis showed that these variables correlated with the average entrainment rate. The multiple variable model was not justified by the observed results.

Although the species assemblage variable improves the predictive ability of the single variable models, the variability is still high. Even the average entrainment rate is very variable within the species assemblages depending on the presence of the specific observations in the data set.

Conclusions of Supplemental Analyses

Although entrainment rates vary among the sites, this variability is not well explained by physical parameters or species composition. There are some broad associations in entrainment rates for groups of related variables, but these do not necessarily indicate a cause-effect relationship. Also, the data set we used is limited in size and includes a number of sites with entrainment rates that are considerably greater or less than those observed from other sites with similar species composition and physical conditions. The data set also contains some groups of sites with relatively similar entrainment rates, physical conditions, and species assemblages.

From these analyses we conclude that the available data *cannot* be used to produce quantitative and statistically significant trends between total entrainment rates and evaluated variables. This does not, however, necessarily preclude estimating entrainment rates at unsampled sites.

3.2.6 Analysis of Monthly Trends of Representative Species

Although there were no definitive trends in the statistical trend analysis using total annual entrainment rates, there may be species-specific monthly trends. We plotted the monthly entrainment rate for representative species for sites within watersheds with more than two entrainment studies included in the database. Any monthly species-specific trends were considered most likely to be evident within the same watershed. Species-specific monthly entrainment rates for additional sites were considered as warranted by the base analysis. Because, for clupeids, monthly entrainment data were only available for a limited number of projects, we presented all available monthly data regardless of watershed location.

Smallmouth Bass

Figure 3-6 shows the monthly entrainment rate of smallmouth bass within the two Michigan drainage basins. Smallmouth entrainment, which occurs between May and October, is generally less than two fish/hour. Entrainment rates of smallmouth bass increased in October at the Muskegon River sites and at Cooke and Foote on the Au Sable River. This is most likely attributable to increased mobility of young-of-the-year. There was no such increase at the other four Au Sable River sites. The only available parameter that distinguishes Cooke and Foote from the

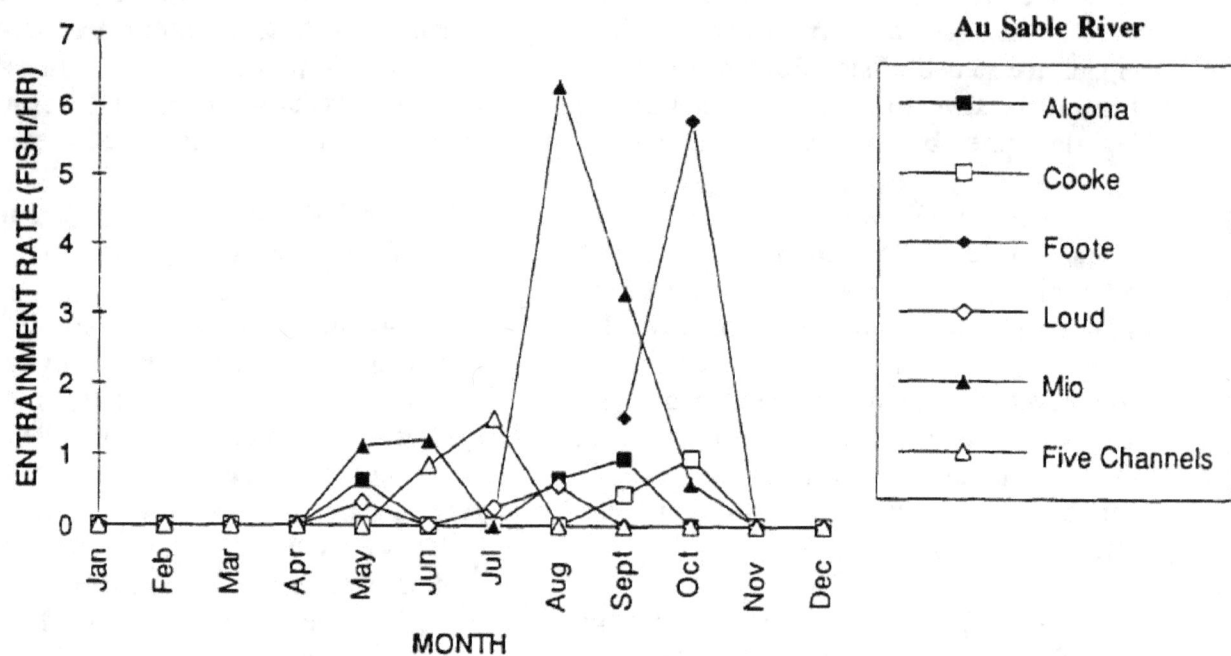

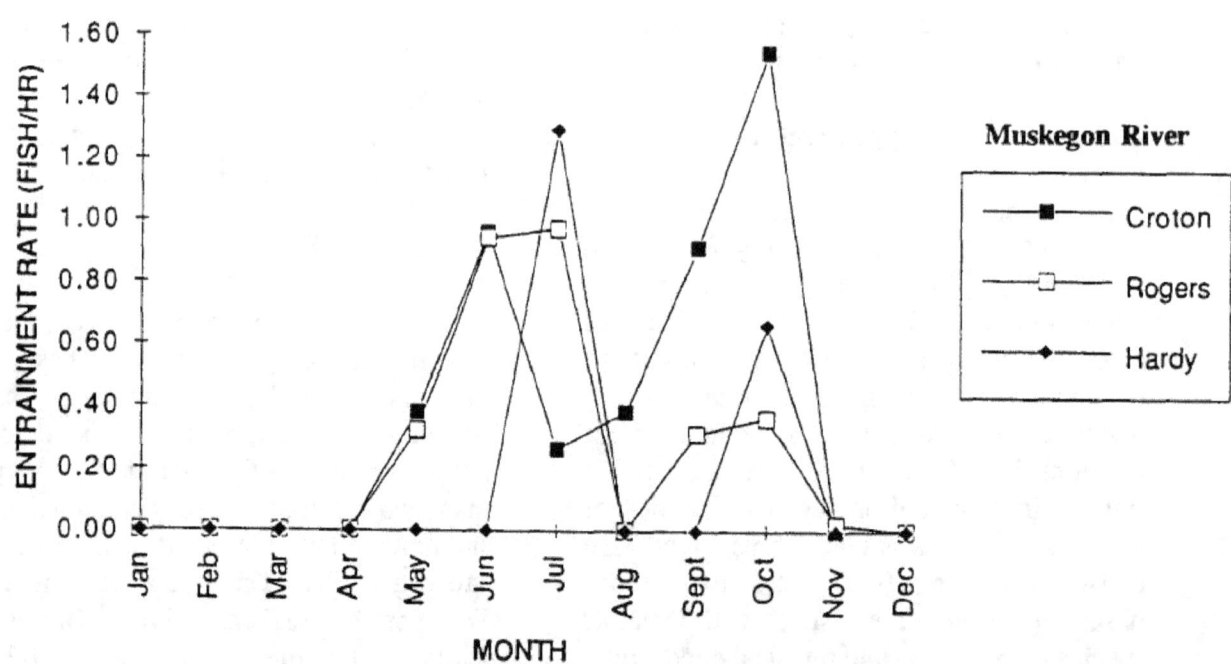

Figure 3-6
Smallmouth Bass Entrainment at Michigan Sites

other Au Sable River sites is that the size of both reservoirs (1,800 acres) is 725 acres larger than any of the other reservoirs in this basin. The Muskegon River sites do not have uniformly large reservoirs, however, reservoir size does not seem to be related to the fall peak of smallmouth bass entrainment rates. Other than the fall trend, there is no consistency in entrainment rate; entrainment rates increase at some sites as they decrease or remain the same at other sites.

Seasonal trends in the entrainment rate of smallmouth bass were more consistent at the Wisconsin sites (Figure 3-7) where most entrainment occurs between May and October. There is a uniform peak in entrainment rates at all three sites in June, however, that may correlate with increased movement of juveniles and adults to preferred habitat. The magnitude of the peak is dramatically different: 0.37/hour at Brule, 1.75/hour at White Rapids, and 27.3/hour at Wisconsin River Division. (The mesh in the rear half of the net used at Wisconsin River Division was smaller than the other two sites, which probably resulted in the collection of more small fish.) The depth to the top of the intake is 22 feet at Brule, 7.5 feet at White Rapids, and 0 feet at Wisconsin River Division, which suggests that deeper intakes may exclude smallmouth bass in June.

To further explore this relationship, we examined monthly entrainment rates at two additional Wisconsin sites, Shawano and Crowley. There was a slight peak in the June smallmouth entrainment rate at both sites (0.30/hour and 0.80/hour, respectively). The depth to the top of the intake at both of these sites was 3 feet. A cause-effect relationship between intake depth and smallmouth bass entrainment rates cannot be determined conclusively based on the limited data. Another peak in smallmouth entrainment rates occurred in September at the Menominee watershed sites as well as at Shawano, possibly corresponding to the increased vulnerability of young-of-the-year. There was no increase at Wisconsin River Division or Crowley.

In general, seasonal peaks in smallmouth entrainment rates may be predicted at some sites. The magnitude of such peaks, however, appears to be unpredictable.

Walleye

There is no consistent trend in monthly entrainment rates of walleye at the Michigan sites either in seasonality or magnitude (Figure 3-8). There is some increased entrainment during the spring at some sites, which may be an artifact of tailrace intrusion of adults into the partial-flow tailrace nets.

Entrainment rates of walleye at three of the four Wisconsin sites in the Menominee and Wisconsin River basins peaked during June. A fourth site (Brule) showed a distinct peak during July (Figure 3-9). Two of the four Wisconsin sites exhibited a minor peak during October, probably corresponding to increased vulnerability of young walleye due to die-off of vegetation that keeps young fish in nursery areas. The magnitude of the June/July entrainment rate peaks at Park Mill, Brule, and Rothschild, ranging from 4.40 to 5.30 walleye/hour seem consistent. A review of late spring/early summer walleye entrainment rates at other Wisconsin sites showed much greater variability. At Thornapple, the peak entrainment rate (in May) was 1.1 fish/hour and the peak entrainment rate at Crowley (in June) was 16.7 fish/hour.

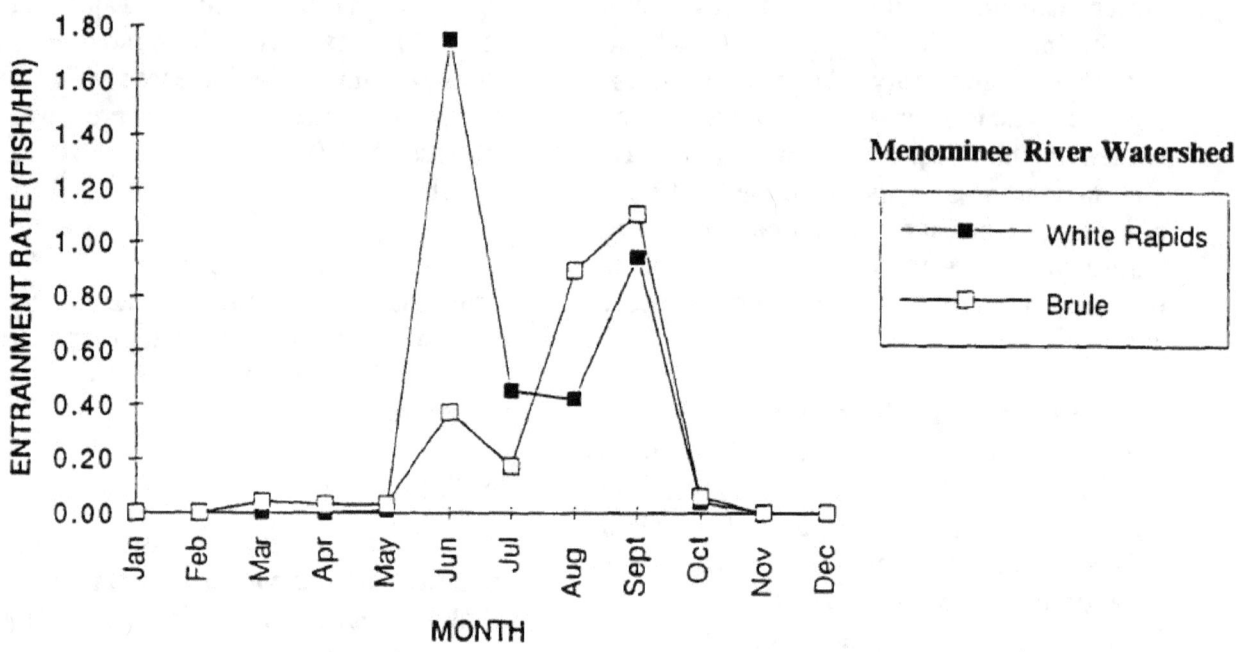

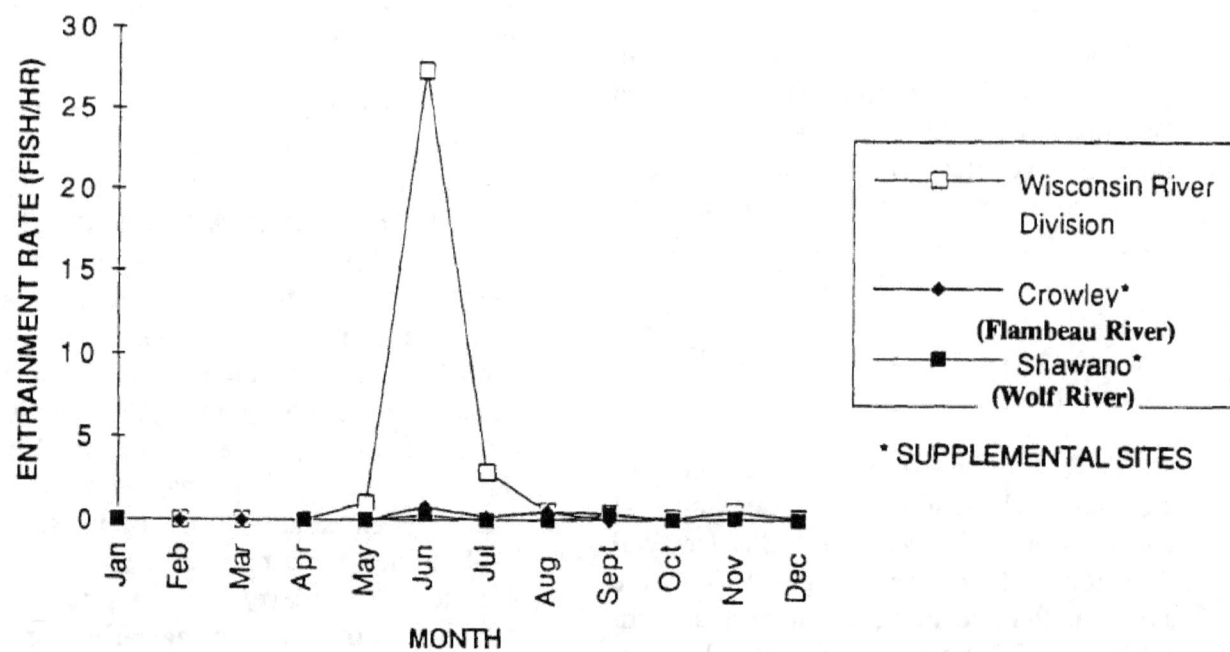

Figure 3-7
Smallmouth Bass Entrainment at Wisconsin Sites

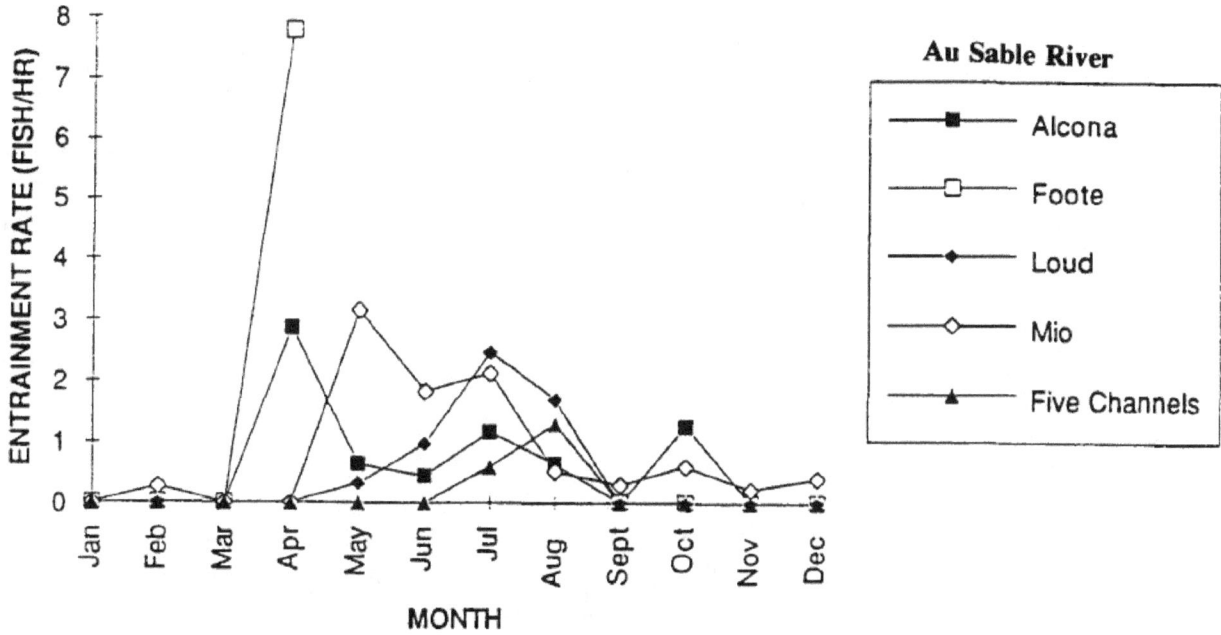

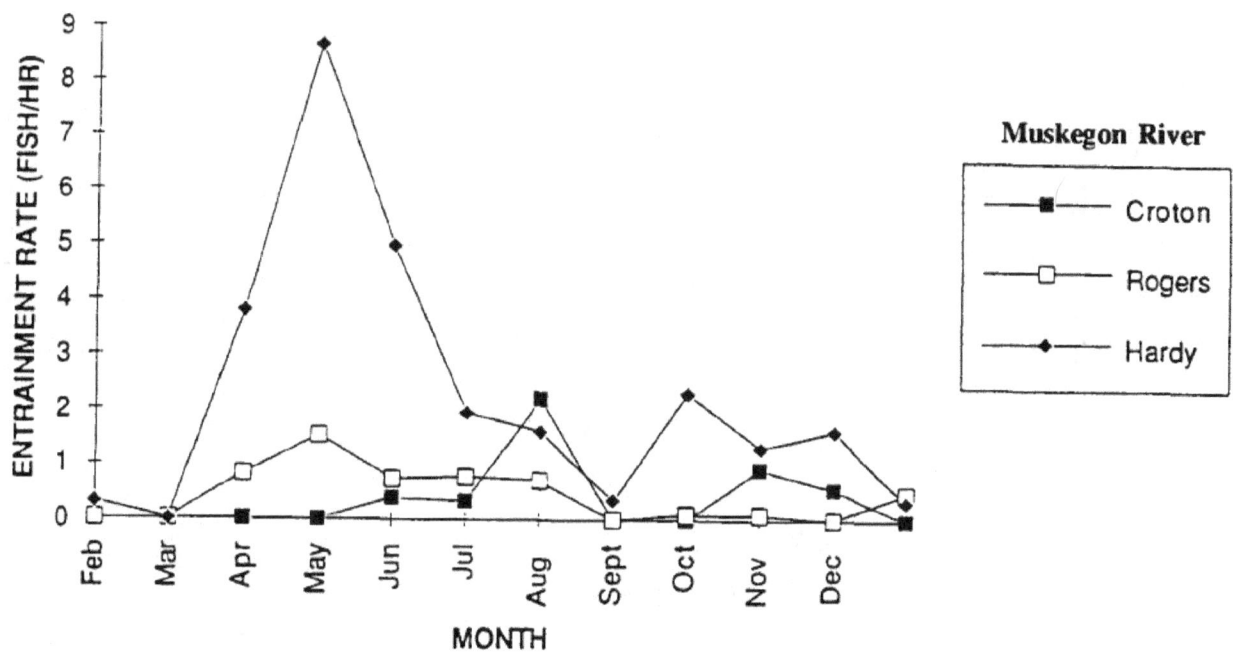

Figure 3-8
Walleye Entrainment at Michigan Sites

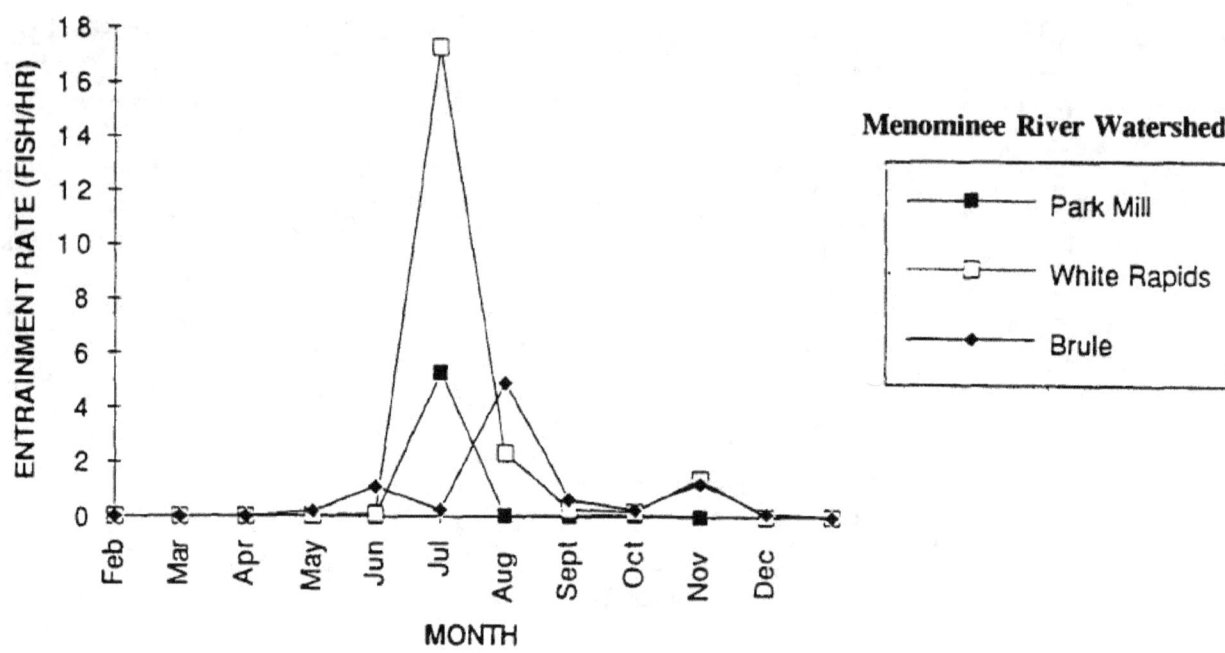

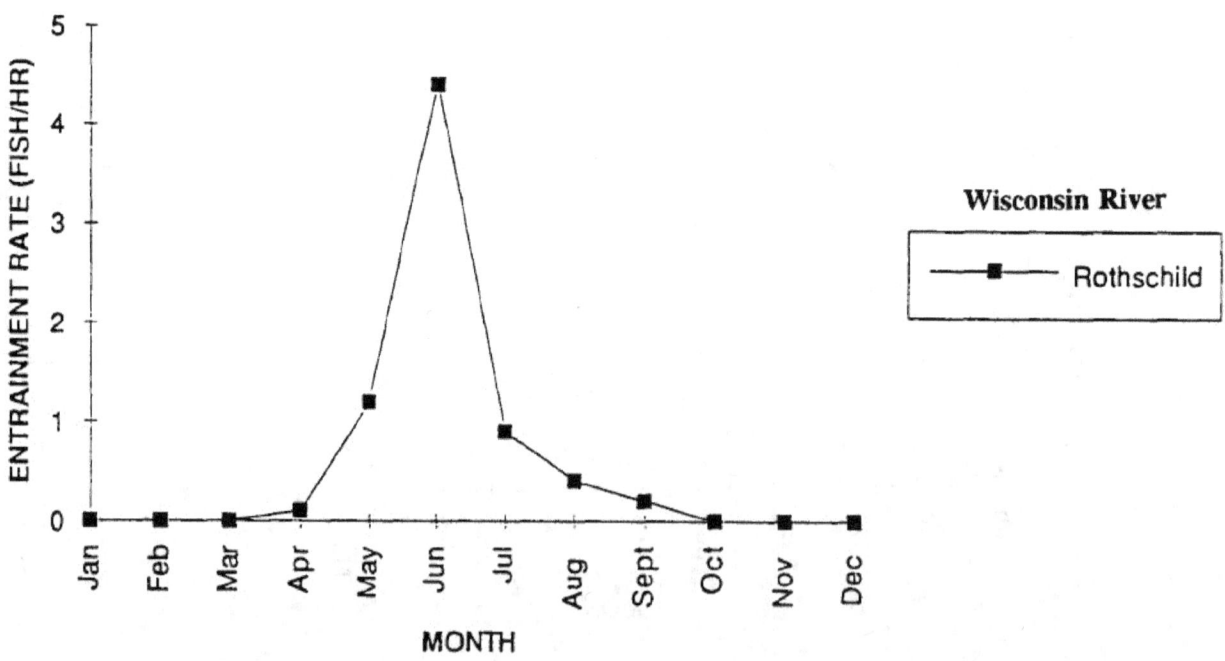

Figure 3-9
Walleye Entrainment at Wisconsin Sites

We compared the physical characteristics of the two sites with comparatively high June/July entrainment rates, White Rapids and Crowley, to those with much lower peak walleye entrainment rates. The trashrack spacing at White Rapids and Crowley was 2.4 to 2.5 inches, whereas at Brule, Rothschild, and Thornapple the trashrack spacing was 1.4 to 1.7 inches, suggesting that the narrower spacing of trashracks may correlate to the lower entrainment rates. This relationship is not evident at the Park Mill Project, which has trashrack spacing of 3.0 inches, but walleye entrainment rates comparable to Brule and Rothschild.

Black Crappie

Entrainment of black crappie at Michigan sites generally increases after March and decreases after November (Figure 3-10). Within this time frame, there are peaks at some sites (i.e., there are entrainment rate peaks in June and November at Cooke, Croton, and Hardy) but little discernable peaks at the other Michigan sites. A review of limited physical characteristics of these plants reveals no apparent reason for these intersite differences. The entrainment rate of black crappie was also inconsistent at two other Michigan sites, Prickett and French Landing. At Prickett, the black crappie peak entrainment rate occurred during April (35.7/hour) while at French Landing (where over 75 percent of entrained fish were black crappie), peaks in total entrainment occurred in July (774.4/hour) and November (610.2/hour).

The peak black crappie entrainment rate noted at some Michigan sites in June seems to shift to July or August at most of the sites in the Wisconsin River and Menominee basins (Figure 3-11). There

were minor peaks at some Wisconsin sites during October (White Rapids) and November (Wisconsin River Division), but too few black crappie were collected at Park Mill to reveal any trends at this site. The peak summer entrainment rate at Rothschild (33.4 fish/hour) is approximately four times greater than at the other two sites on the Wisconsin River. The most obvious difference between these sites is the size of the Rothschild impoundment, which is more than six times larger than the other two impoundments.

We compared black crappie entrainment at sites within the Broad River watershed in the southeast with midwestern sites to look for similar trends. At all three sites with more than incidental black crappie entrainment, there was a fall peak (Figure 3-12), most likely reflecting increased vulnerability of young fish. This peak occurred during September and October at Hollidays Bridge, during October and November at Ninety-nine Islands, and during November at Saluda. These fall peaks appear analogous to the fall peaks noted at midwestern sites.

At Hollidays Bridge there was a winter peak during December and January, but not at the other two sites. The intake of the Hollidays Bridge Project is 19 feet deep, but only 13 and 8 feet deep at Saluda and Ninety-nine Islands. This deeper intake may favor entrainment of fish during periods of relative inactivity and cooler water temperatures.

Yellow Perch

There were few consistent trends in entrainment of yellow perch at most sites in the Au Sable watershed (Figure 3-13). Spring and fall peaks were evident at Cooke and a slight peak in April at Alcona and

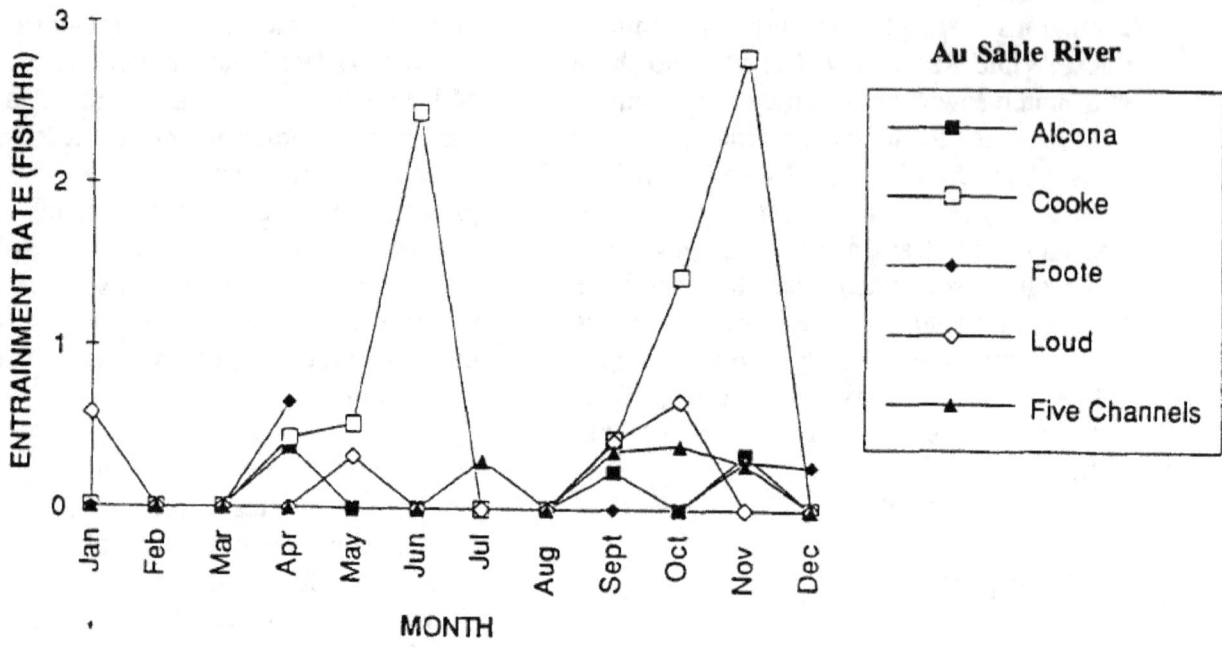

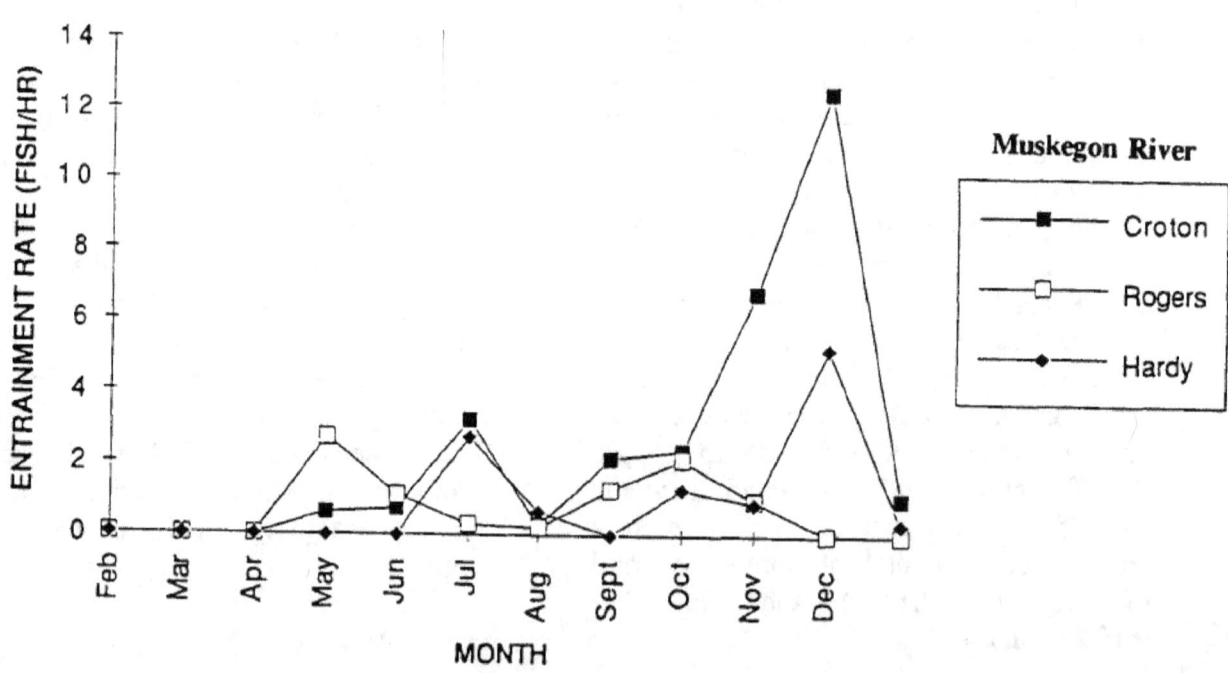

Figure 3-10
Black Crappie Entrainment at Michigan Sites

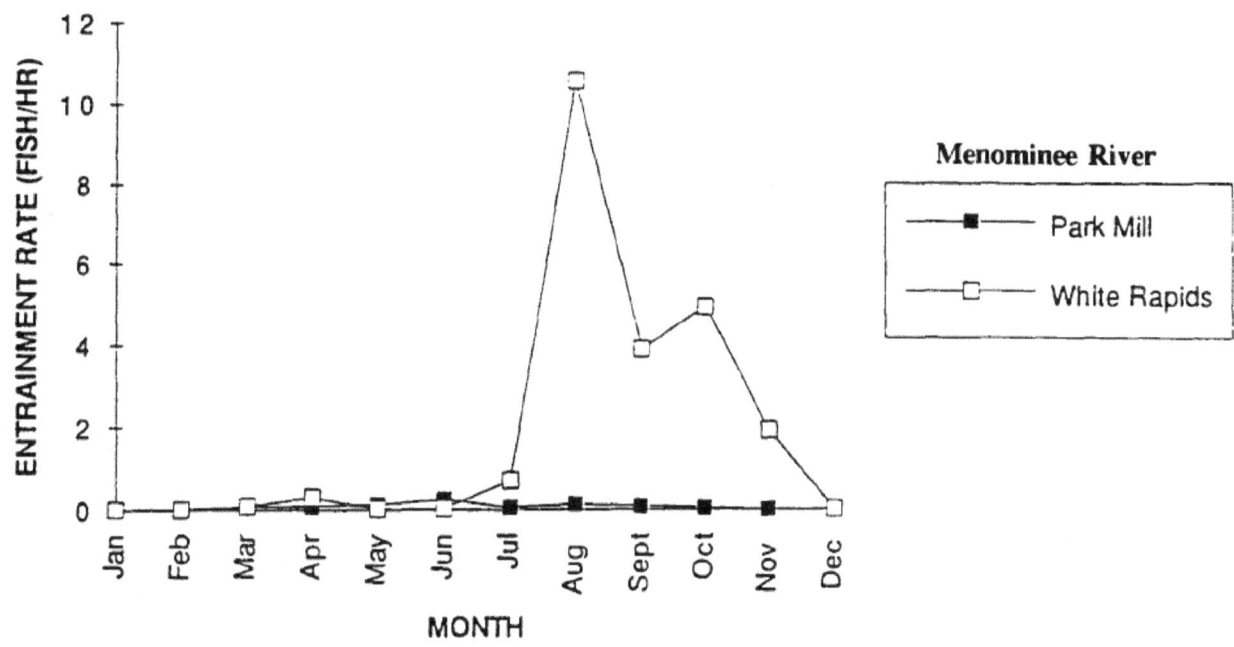

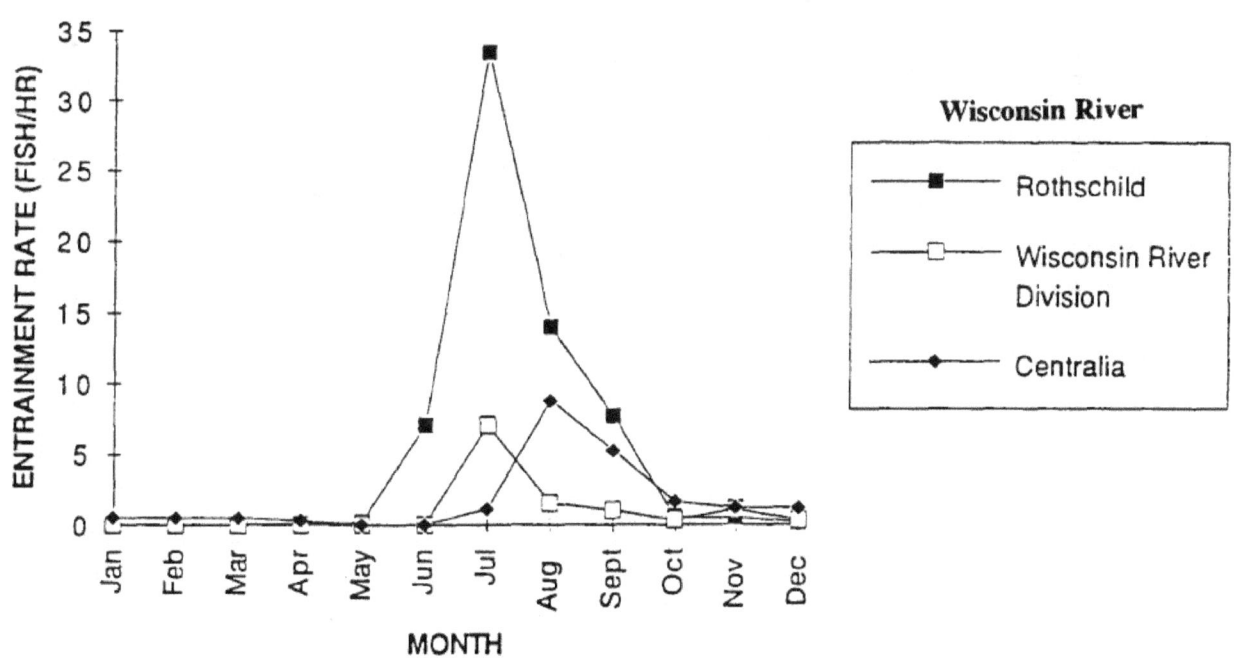

Figure 3-11
Black Crappie Entrainment at Wisconsin Sites

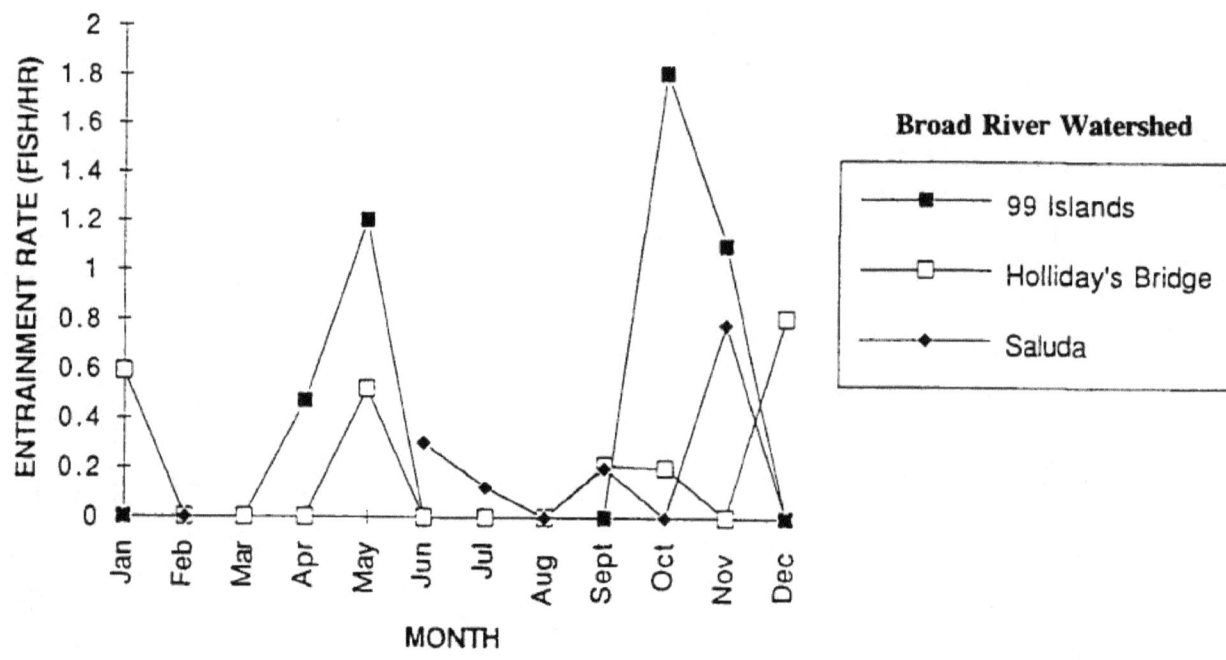

Figure 3-12
Black Crappie Entrainment at South Carolina Sites

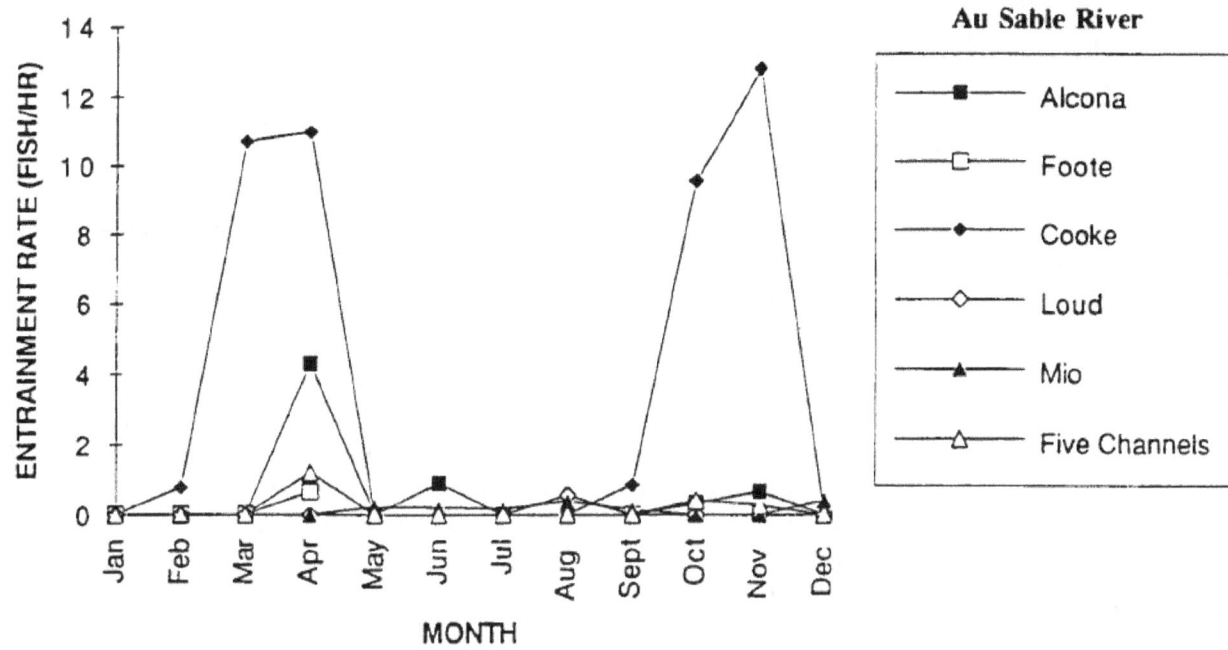

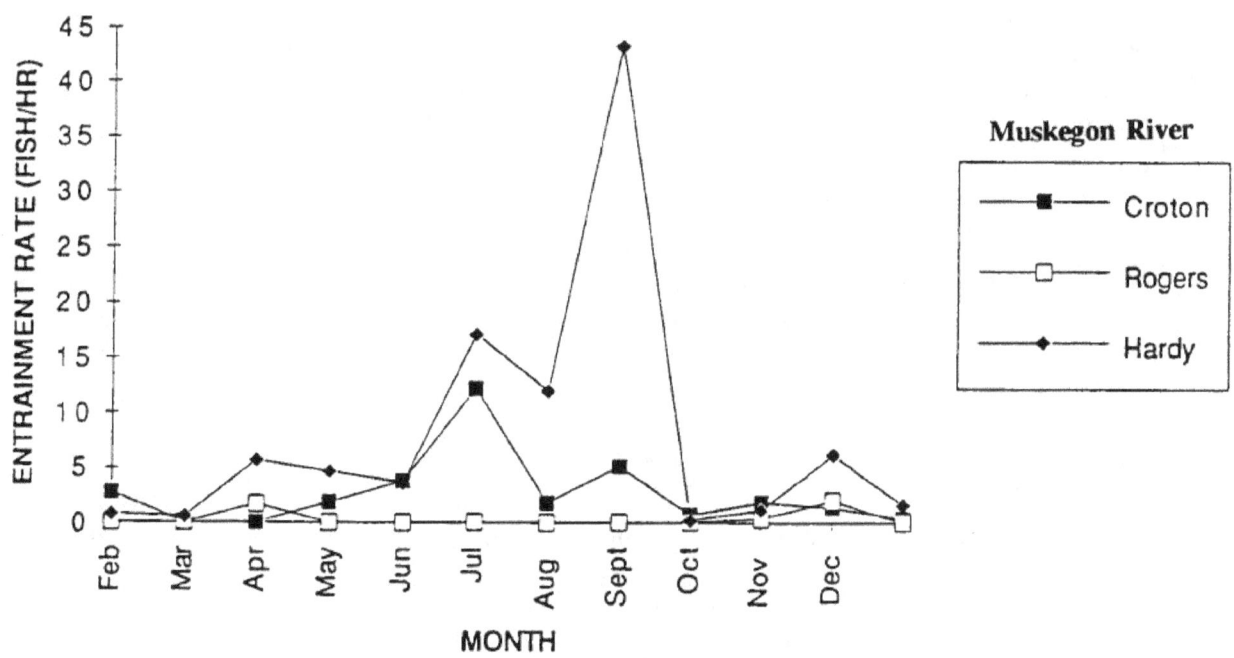

Figure 3-13
Yellow Perch Entrainment at Michigan

Five Channels. In contrast, the pattern at Croton and Hardy on the Muskegon River showed a peak in June and August, with a minor peak at Hardy in November.

There was a major peak in entrainment rates at Brule and White Rapids in June and/or July (Figure 3-14), with a secondary peak at both sites in October. The average size of yellow perch at Brule was 1.2 inches and at White Rapids, 2.0 inches, suggesting that nearly all yellow perch entrained at these two sites were young-of-the-year.

Entrainment rates at Buzzard's Roost were substantially greater than at any other site in the database (Figure 3-15). After the peak entrainment rate (86.4 fish/hour) in April, numbers declined substantially. Saluda was the only other site within the Broad watershed at which yellow perch comprised more than an incidental portion of the entrainment catch. There was no entrainment sampling by net at Saluda during March, April, and May, and, therefore, it is not possible to determine if this spring peak also occurred here. Monthly entrainment rates were plotted for Abbeville, which is in proximity to the Broad watershed, as a supplemental analysis to assess whether the spring peak at Buzzard's Roost was an anomaly. Abbeville showed a spring peak in March rather than April, but the magnitude of the peak at Abbeville was a third of that at Buzzard's Roost. The only other southern site at which yellow perch were collected was King Mill. Monthly data at this site reveal a very slight peak in March (1.1 fish/hour) although sampling was not conducted in January or February.

In general, peak entrainment rates of yellow perch vary in different regions. The magnitude of peak entrainment events also varied, except for the June/July peak at White Rapids and Brule.

White Sucker

The estimated entrainment rates for white sucker at the Michigan sites on the Au Sable and Muskegon rivers were strongly influenced by the intrusion of fish into the partial-flow tailrace nets, especially during the localized spring spawning migration. Most fish collected were more than 10 inches long, much larger than most fish collected with full-flow nets. Because of this intrusion, monthly entrainment rates presented in Figure 3-16 should be interpreted cautiously.

Entrainment rates of white sucker at the two Menominee watershed sites, Brule and Park Mill, were never higher than 0.6 fish/hour (Figure 3-17). There was a peak at Brule during June, comprised mostly of fish believed to be 1 year old based on monthly size distribution data. There are no other trends in white sucker entrainment rates.

Clupeids

Because clupeids normally travel in dense schools, sometimes they can be entrained in high numbers. As previously discussed, clupeid entrainment is often episodic (e.g., alewife entrainment at the Youghiogheny Project). Monthly entrainment rates for gizzard shad and threadfin shad are discussed in the following section (monthly data for other clupeids are not readily available). Entrainment was generally dominated by young fish from 1.5 to 4.0 inches in length, but in some cases included fish up to 14 inches in length.

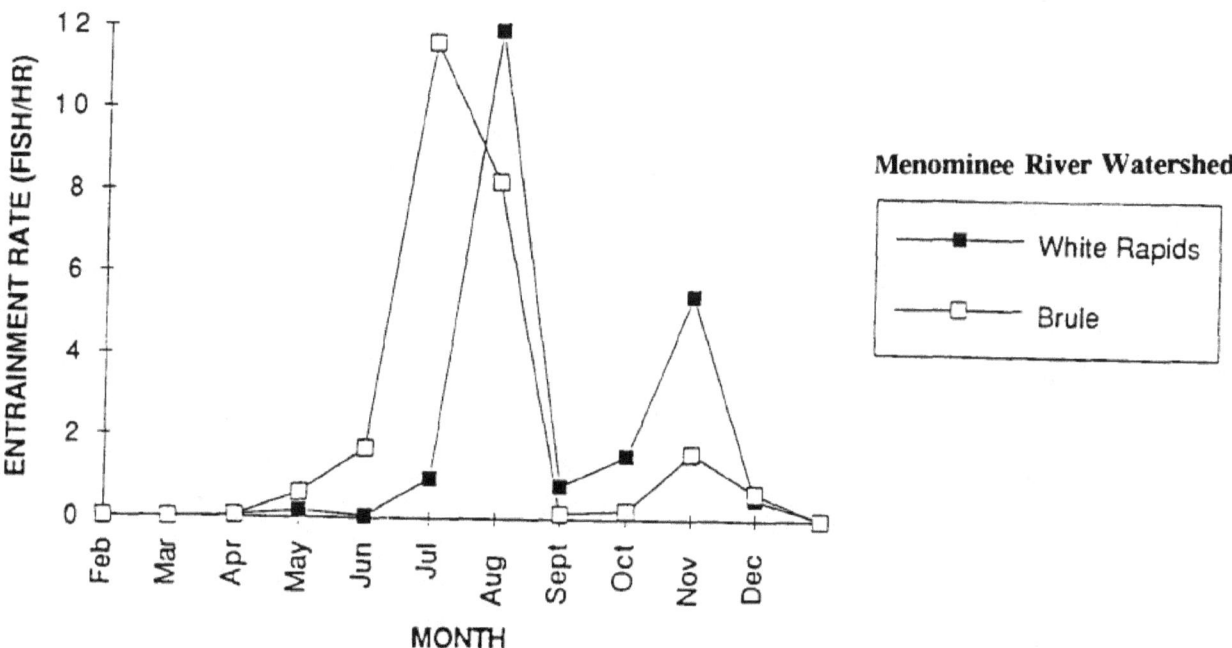

Figure 3-14
Yellow Perch Entrainment at Wisconsin Sites

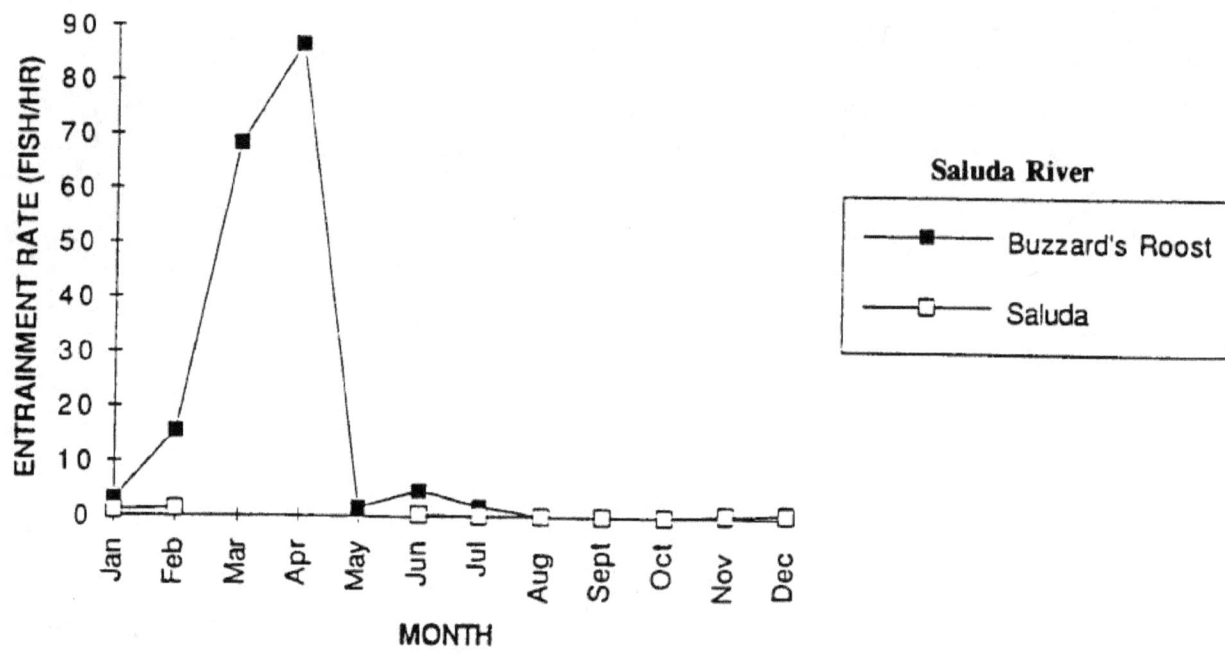

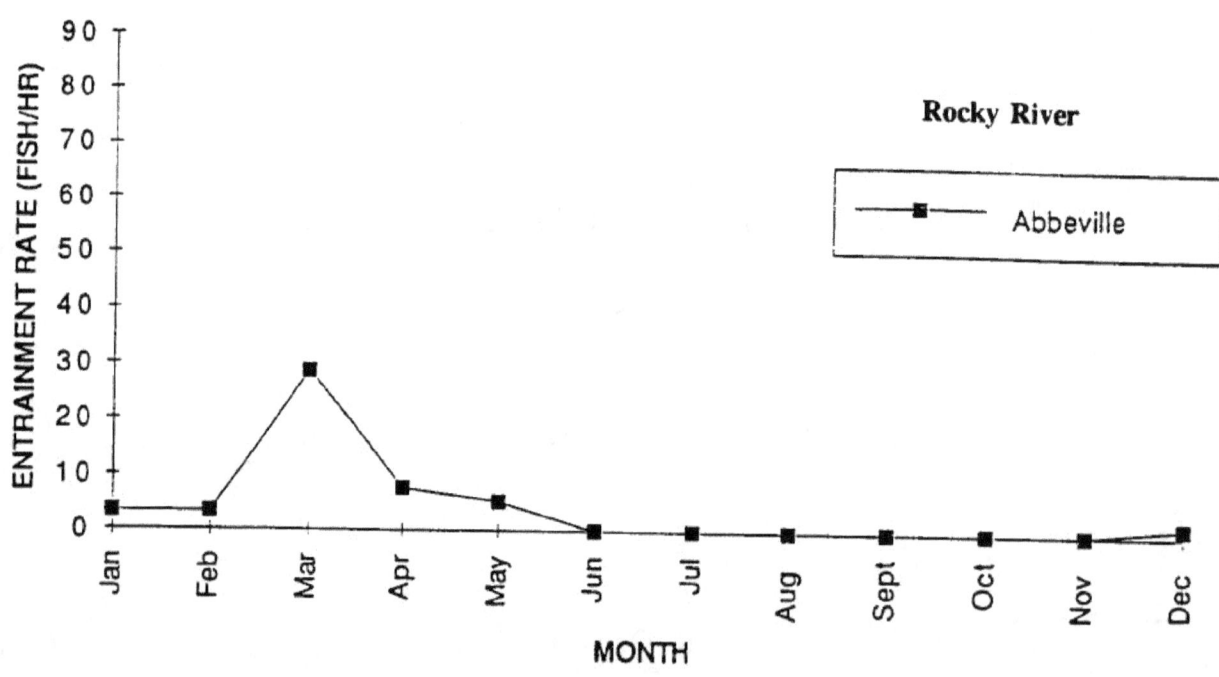

Figure 3-15
Yellow Perch Entrainment at South Carolina Sites

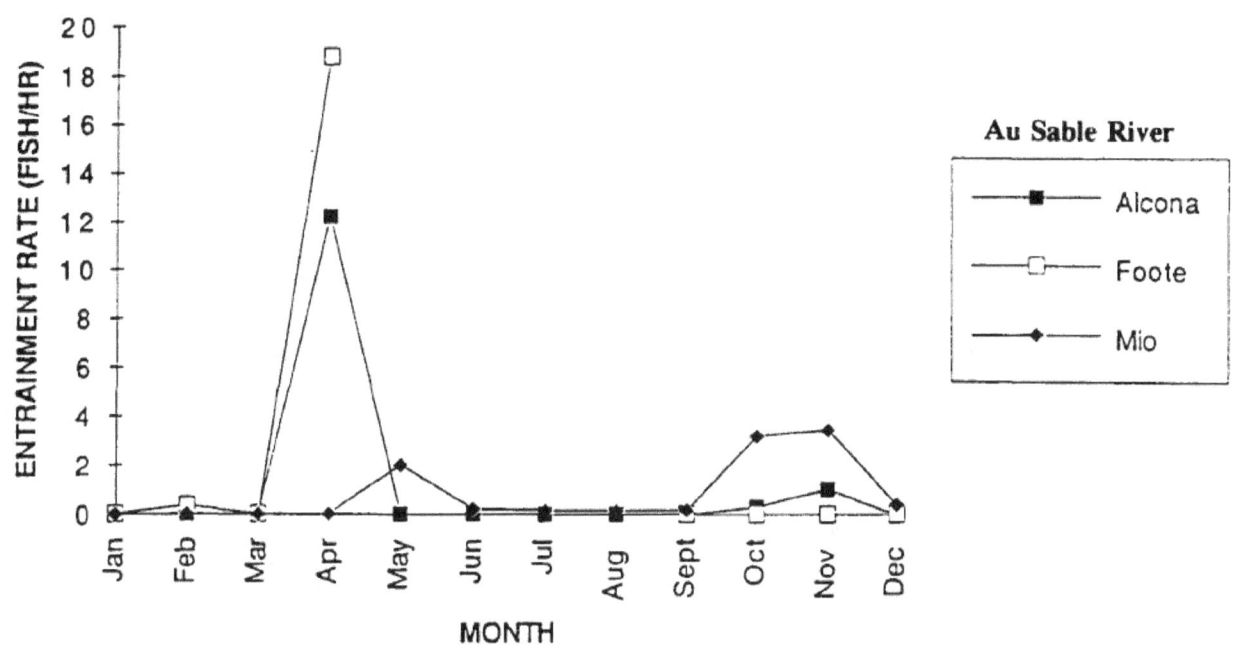

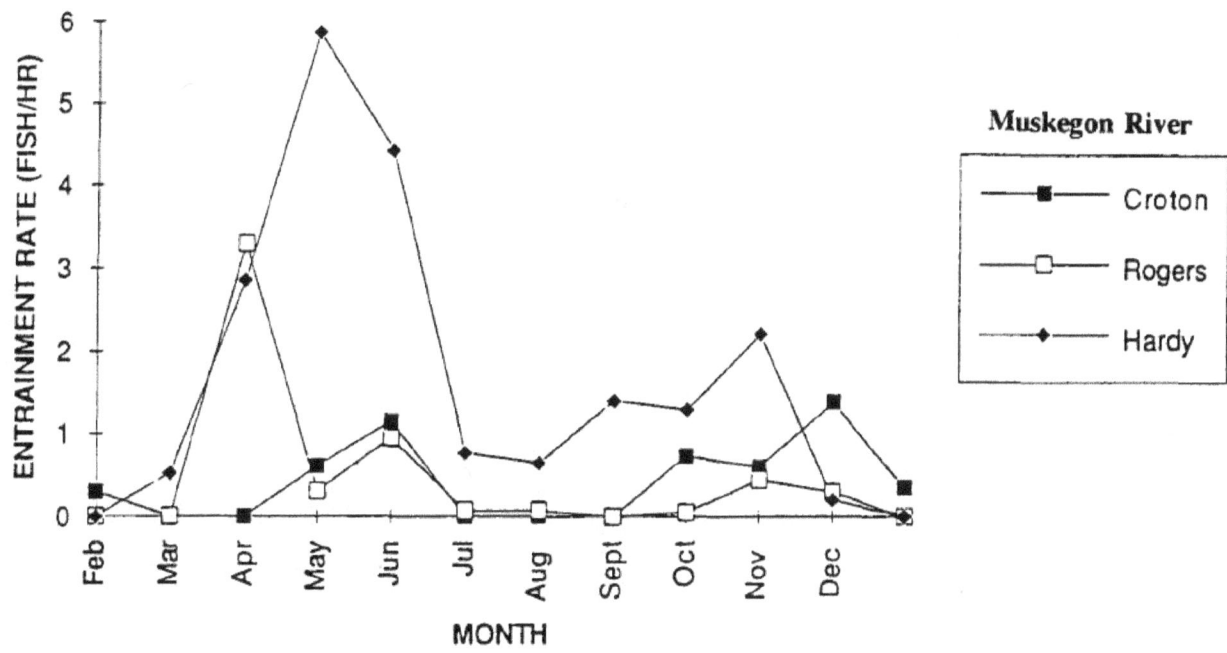

Figure 3-16
White Sucker Entrainment at Michigan Sites

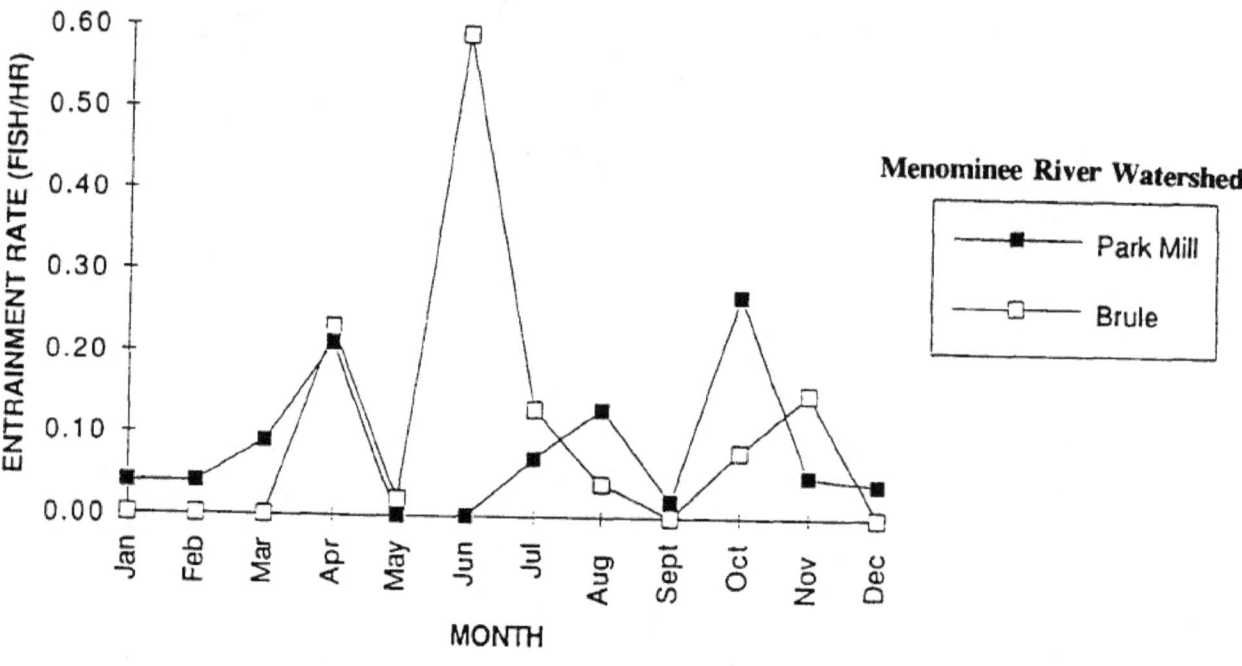

Figure 3-17
White Sucker Entrainment at Wisconsin Sites

The most prevalent seasonal trend in gizzard shad entrainment at many sites is the fall (usually October and/or November) peak in abundance (Figures 3-18 and 3-19). This peak is quite pronounced at some sites: 25.8 fish/hour at Hawks Nest; 49.6 fish/hour at Lock and Dam No. 2; and 5,930 fish/hour at Greenup Lock and Dam (the latter was not graphed because of the relative difference with other sites and there were only two other data points for the year). These three sites each have average river flows in excess of 9,000 cfs.

The remaining six sites with enough entrained gizzard shad to evaluate have average river flows of less than 2,500 cfs. There is no fall peak at Croton, Gaston Shoals, or King Mill; at Saluda peak entrainment begins in November but continues at least through February (Figure 3-19). Hollidays Bridge has a similar but less pronounced cool weather increase in the entrainment rate during December and January.

Entrainment of gizzard shad during the spring and summer generally ranged from 0 to 6.9 fish/hour with the exception of Greenup Lock and Dam, where the spring rate was 86.3 fish/hour. Greenup also illustrates the temporal variability that is frequently evident in clupeid entrainment rates, as none were collected in the summer sampling effort. Lock and Dam No. 2 also shows temporal variability with monthly entrainment rates from December to August varying from 0 to approximately 4 fish/hour.

Threadfin shad were only represented at sites in South Carolina and Georgia (Figure 3-20). The entrainment rate of threadfin shad at Buzzard's Roost is dramatically greater than any other site or any other species, with the maximum rate of 13,622 fish/hour occurring in February. The high winter entrainment rates are inconsistent across sites; winter peaks may be due to low water temperature stress. Most sites exhibit a spring peak in entrainment of clupeids. The Buzzard's Roost impoundment (11,404 acres) is larger than any other impoundment included in the database except Lock and Dam No. 2, which is 11,810 acres.

3.2.7 Size Composition Assessment

Evaluating the size of entrained fish is complicated by variable approaches to reporting this information (see discussion in Section 3.2.1). In general, however, mostly small fish are entrained. We assessed the size of entrained fish at each site by establishing three groupings: sites strongly dominated by small fish (75 percent or more of the entrained fish are 4 inches or less); sites strongly dominated by small to moderate sized fish (75 percent or more of the entrained fish are 6 inches or less); and sites with variable-sized fish (the remaining sites). We evaluated size of entrained fish for 40 of the 45 sites included in the database.

Twelve sites were dominated by small fish (Table 3-5). We included three sites in this category based on hydroacoustic target strength data (Tower, Kleber, and White Rapids), even though net-derived size-distribution data indicate that these sites have more variable- (Tower) or moderately-sized fish. (The executive summaries for the studies at these three sites presented only the hydroacoustic size distribution, so we concluded that these data are more representative.) Eleven sites were dominated by small to moderate-sized fish, and 17 sites had more variable-sized fish. Of the 17 sites in the latter category, however, 10 are based on size distribution

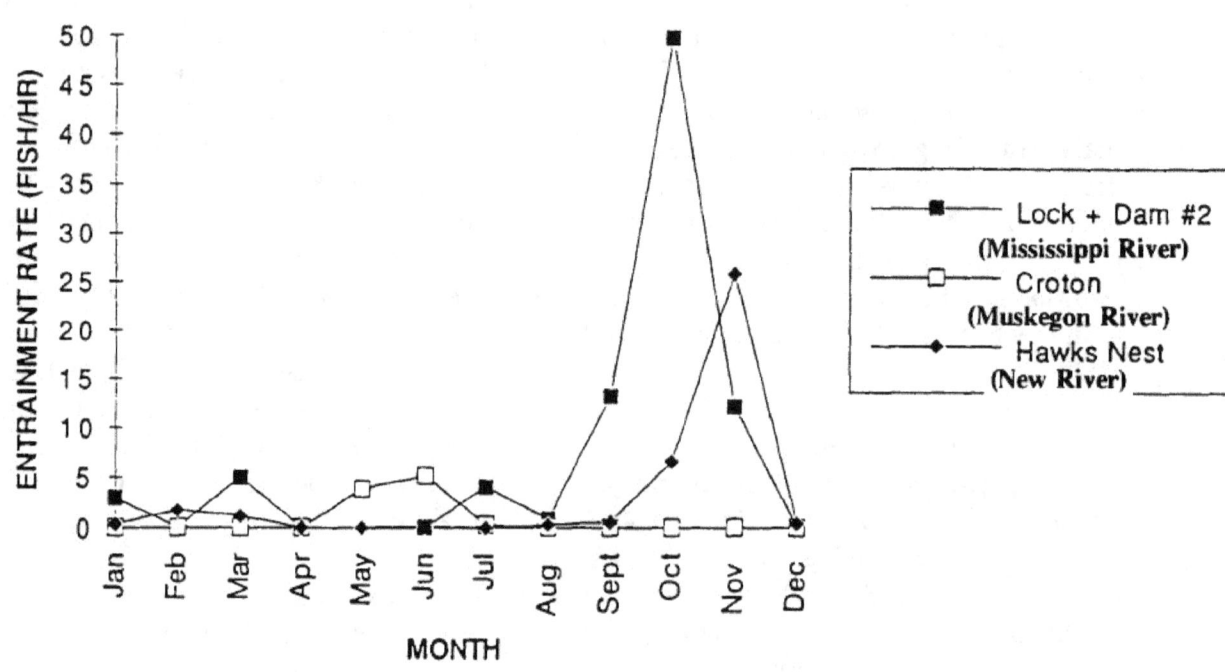

Figure 3-18
Gizzard Shad Entrainment at Midwestern Sites
and West Virginia

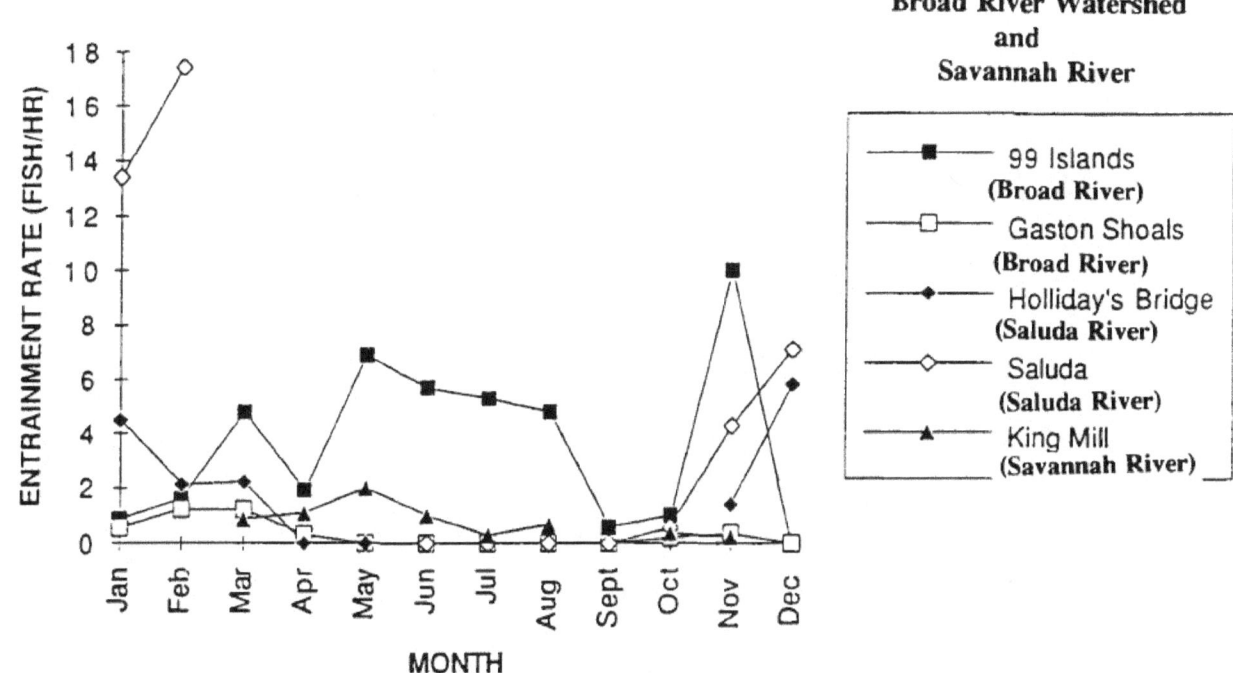

Figure 3-19
Gizzard Shad Entrainment at Southeastern Sites
(Georgia and South Carolina)

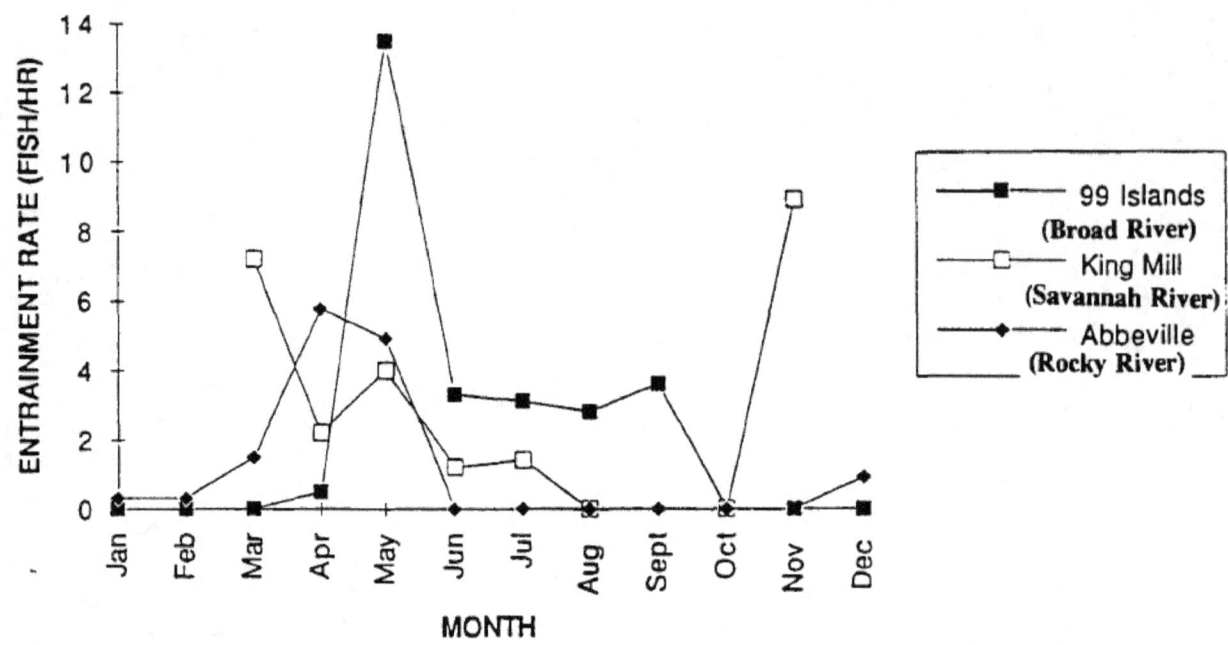

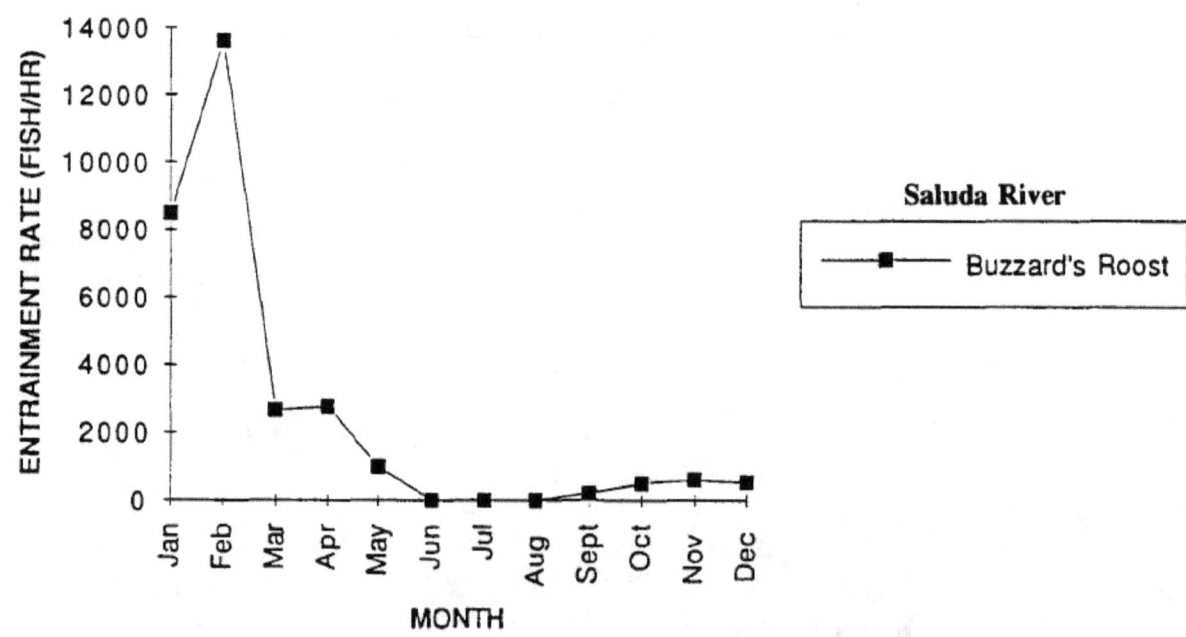

Figure 3-20
Threadfin Shad Entrainment at Southeastern Sites
(Georgia and South Carolina)

TABLE 3-5 PREDOMINANT SIZE OF ENTRAINED FISH AT SITES INCLUDED IN THE DATABASE		
Sites Dominated by Small Fish ($\geq 75\% \leq 4.0$ inches)	Sites Dominated by Small to Moderate Sized Fish ($\geq 75\% \leq 6.0$ inches)	Sites Dominated by Large Fish (all remaining sites)
Tower (89%- HA)	Escanaba Dam 3 (75%)	Alcona*
Kleber (95%- HA)	Thornapple (80%)	Foote*
Prickett (84%)	King Mill (95%)*	Cooke*
Park Mill (79%)*	Brule (86%)	Loud*
Crowley (78%)	Escanaba Dam 1	Mio*
White Rapids (82%- HA)	Shawano	Five Channels*
Centralia (97%)	Abbeville*	Croton*
Rothschild	Greenup Lock and Dam*	Rogers*
Wisconsin River Division	Station 26	Hardy*
Youghiogheny	Buchanan*	Moores Park
Hawks Nest*	Constantine	French Landing*
Buzzard's Roost		99 Islands
		Gaston Shoals
		Saluda
		Hollidays Bridge
		Dam No. 4
		Millville

* All or part of the entrainment estimate derived from partial flow netting.

Note: All size characterizations based on netting data unless marked by "HA" (for hydroacoustics). When readily calculated, size percentages indicated in parenthesis; otherwise, size categorizations based on best available evidence.

information data derived from partial-flow tailrace netting. This method may overestimate the presence of larger fish because of tailrace intrusion.

We did not detect from our analysis a relationship between trashrack bar spacing and size of entrained fish. However, one would expect that fish wider than the trashrack clear bar spacing would be excluded from entrainment. Bar spacing at Moores Park is 1.62 inches and at Dam No. 4 is 1.25 inches; both of these sites entrained relatively large fish based on full-flow tailrace netting.

Tower has the smallest trashrack spacing of all projects included in the database. The 1-inch trashrack in place at this site is frequently recommended as an entrainment protective measure. If this trashrack successfully excludes larger fish, then the entrainment catch at this site should be comprised almost entirely of small fish. The trashracks at Kleber have 3-inch spacing. The same consultant conducted the entrainment studies at both sites. Because the methods used at both sites are comparable, we can assess the influence of trashrack width on the size of entrained fish. There were some differences in the relative abundance of species entrained at the two sites (darters were dominant at Tower), however, which may have a bearing on the size composition of entrained fish. The hydroacoustic target size of entrained fish at Tower indicated that 89 percent were less than 3.9 inches. At Kleber, however, the target size data indicated that more smaller-sized fish (95 percent of the total) were entrained.

These results suggest that the size of entrained fish was similar at Tower and Kleber in spite of the differing trashrack spacing. The entrainment rate at Tower (3.4 fish/hour) was approximately half that at Kleber (7.2 fish/hour), although this may have been related to differences in species composition and trashrack spacing.

3.3 Comparison of Entrainment to Reservoir Populations

Much of the potential impact of entrainment and turbine mortality is to the fish community within the impoundment at the hydropower project. Many entrainment studies contain information on the impoundment communities including relative abundance of different species within the impoundment and several present actual population estimates of selected target species. Comparing these data to the entrainment data provides insight into the relationship of entrainment to the potentially entrained fish community.

It often is difficult to compare relative abundances and population sizes among sites because of different methods used to evaluate populations. The relative abundance of fish in impoundments on the Au Sable and Muskegon rivers used five different collection methods (electrofishing, fyke nets, seines, gill nets and trap nets); relative abundance data for the White Rapids impoundment were obtained using only fyke nets. The Centralia relative abundance data are based on electrofishing data. All approaches provide useful information, but data collected at one site are not necessarily comparable to another site because of different gear selection, i.e., gear is both size- and species-selective. Similarly, the population of forage-sized fish (<150 mm long) at Buzzard's Roost was estimated hydroacoustically whereas the other four sites at which population estimates were available were based on mark and recapture studies that focused on fish more than 1 year old.

Gear selectivity can also bias comparisons of relative or actual abundance of species in the impoundments with entrainment rates. Partial-flow netting, such as at the Au Sable and Muskegon sites, also may affect relative abundance accuracy of entrainment studies. Tables 3-6 to 3-9 present comparisons of impoundment populations with commonly entrained fish.

The relative abundance of all species of clupeids was consistently greater in entrainment samples compared to the impoundment populations at both sites where data were available. Conversely, the relative abundance of brown and black bullheads was always greater in the impoundments compared to the entrainment samples (six comparisons).

Several species showed trends of generally greater relative abundance in entrainment samples compared to their respective impoundments. These species are channel catfish (3 of 4 comparisons), smallmouth bass (6 of 8 comparisons), black crappie (7 of 9 comparisons), bluegill (9 of 13 comparisons), and walleye (8 of 9 comparisons). The relative abundance of minnows was generally greater in impoundments than in entrainment samples (9 of 15 comparisons). The relative abundance of rock bass at sites on the Au Sable River was quite similar at 5 of the 6 sites. All of these comparisons are heavily influenced by the results of entrainment studies that used partial-flow netting, so the results probably include intrusion of non-entrained fish.

It is difficult to show trends beyond those indicated due to the limited number of studies with comparable data from impoundment sampling and entrainment sampling with full-flow netting. The species composition of entrainment samples is also likely to be affected by site-specific characteristics unaccounted for in the database (e.g., proximity of the intake to high or low temperature sources and/or nursery and spawning grounds). These factors may obscure patterns of entrainment relative to impoundment populations.

Population estimates for target species are available for the impoundments of five projects (Table 3-10). Estimates for four of these projects (Crowley, Rothschild, Wisconsin River Division, and Centralia) are based on mark-recapture studies of fish at least 1 year old and, for the most part, susceptible to being caught by anglers. The average size of most entrained fish of these target species is 1 to 2 inches. Comparing the estimated population to the number of annually entrained individuals of that species indicates the density of harvestable fish in the impoundment that can be achieved in spite of the indicated levels of entrainment of young fish.

Entrainment at Crowley was dominated by young walleye (23,311 individuals; average size: 1.5 inches). The impoundment supports an estimated population of 19 walleye per acre. Population estimates for walleye (all harvestable sizes) in both natural lakes and hydropower impoundments in Wisconsin range from 1.8 to 48.3 per acre (Weyerhaeuser et al., 1993). The density of walleye in the Crowley impoundment represents the fifth highest density of all reported values. Although annual entrainment rates of walleye at the remaining three projects was considerably less, the density of walleyes in these impoundments was lower than that at Crowley.

TABLE 3-6
RELATIVE ABUNDANCE OF DOMINANT SPECIES COLLECTED IN IMPOUNDMENTS COMPARED TO ENTRAINED FISH AT PROJECTS ON THE AU SABLE RIVER, MICHIGAN

Species	Alcona Imp. (%)	Alcona Ent.* (%)	Foote Imp. (%)	Foote Ent. (%)	Cooke Imp. (%)	Cooke Ent. (%)	Loud Imp. (%)	Loud Ent. (%)	Mio Imp. (%)	Mio Ent. (%)	Five Channels Imp. (%)	Five Channels Ent. (%)
Spottail Shiner	--	5.6 (6)	55.5 (1)	--	5.8 (6)	5.8 (5)	5.3 (6)	1.6 (11)	16.4 (2)	--	16.0 (3)	--
Emerald Shiner					31.4 (1)	--						
Bluntnose Minnow											6.1 (5)	--
Shorthead Redhorse							6.6 (5)	--				
Golden Redhorse							14.3 (3)	--				
White Sucker	15.1 (3)	21.5 (2)	--	48.8 (1)			8.3 (4)	--	20.9 (1)	15.9 (3)	10.4 (4)	--
Brown Bullhead	3.9 (4)	--	4.4 (4)	--					12.8 (3)	--		
Channel Catfish			--	2.2 (6)								
Muskelunge					--	9.4 (3)						
Yellow Perch	28.4 (1)	9.6 (5)	12.0 (2)	1.7 (7)	18.9 (2)	54.3 (1)	16.0 (2)	1.6 (11)	6.9 (5)	2.7 (6)	27.6 (1)	6.7 (4)
Walleye	--	10.7 (4)	--	20.0 (2)			--	26.3 (2)	--	15.9 (3)		
Rockbass	28.2 (2)	26.5 (1)	5.3 (3)	6.7 (4)	6.3 (5)	7.2 (4)	19.7 (1)	39.4 (1)	10.1 (4)	19.4 (2)	25.2 (2)	33.3 (1)
Bluegill	--	12.4 (3)					--	8.2 (3)	--	8.2 (5)	--	8.3 (3)
Pumpkinseed			4.0 (5)	--	8.5 (3)	2.2 (7)						
Black Crappie			--	2.7 (5)	8.3 (4)	19.5 (2)	--	8.2 (3)				
Smallmouth Bass	3.9 (5)	3.9 (7)	--	11.1 (3)			--	4.9 (5)	--	27.9 (1)	--	21.7 (2)

*   Relative abundance of entrained fish at all sites on Au Sable River determined by partial flow tailrace netting.

Note: Only dominant species included; dashes indicate incidental catch; numbers in parenthesis indicate species rank. Impoundment populations sampled by electrofishing, fyke net, gill net, seine, and trap net.

TABLE 3-7
RELATIVE ABUNDANCE OF DOMINANT SPECIES COLLECTED IN IMPOUNDMENTS COMPARED TO ENTRAINED FISH AT PROJECTS ON THE MUSKEGON RIVER, MICHIGAN

Species	Croton		Rogers		Hardy	
	Imp. (%)*	Ent. (%)	Imp. (%)	Ent. (%)	Imp. (%)	Ent. (%)
Sea Lamprey	--	5.8 (4)				
Spottail Shiner	71.5 (1)	3.6 (7)	48.3 (1)	4.7 (11)	0.9 (5)	9.3 (4)
Emerald Shiner			6.9 (4)			
Golden Shiner			5.2 (5)			
Common Carp			7.1 (3)			
Fathead Minnow			--	7.4 (4)		
Shorthead Redhorse			--	8.3 (3)		
Silver Redhorse			8.1 (2)	--		
White Sucker					18.2 (2)	14.3 (3)
Channel Catfish			3.8 (7)	--		
Yellow Perch	2.8 (3)	14.9 (2)	--	10.1 (2)	68.5 (1)	37.2 (1)
Walleye			--	6.6 (6)	--	19.8 (2)
Logperch	2.6 (4)	1.3 (14)			9.0 (3)	--
Bluegill	22.6 (2)	34.5 (1)	4.7 (6)	6.0 (8)	1.0 (4)	1.9 (7)
Pumpkinseed	--	4.5 (5)				
Orange Spotted Sunfish	--	3.9 (6)				
Black Crappie	--	13.5 (3)	3.7 (8)	10.8 (1)	--	9.3(5)
Smallmouth Bass	0.2 (5)	1.9 (11)	--	6.8 (5)		

*　　Relative abundance of entrained fish at all sites on the Muskegon River determined by partial-flow tailrace netting.

Note:　Only dominant species included; dashes indicate incidental catch; numbers in parenthesis indicate species rank. Impoundment populations sampled by electrofishing, fyke net, gill net, seine, and trap net. Relative abundance of entrained fish at all sites on Au Sable River determined by partial flow tailrace netting.

TABLE 3-8 (page 1 of 2)
RELATIVE ABUNDANCE OF DOMINANT SPECIES COLLECTED IN IMPOUNDMENTS COMPARED TO ENTRAINED FISH AT MISCELLANEOUS PROJECTS IN MICHIGAN AND WISCONSIN

Species	Buchanan		Constantine		Crowley		Centralia		White Rapids	
	Imp.* (%)	Ent. (%)	Imp. (%)	Ent. (%)	Imp. (%)	Ent. (%)	Imp. (%)	Ent. (%)	Imp. (%)	Ent. (%)
Spotfin Shiner	18.8 (2)	6.3 (4)	7.4 (5)	--						
Mimic Shiner	25.4 (1)	6.3 (4)	--	67.1 (1)						
Sand Shiner	7.0 (3)	2.5 (5)	14.2 (3)	3.4 (4)						
Common Shiner									--	25.6 (1)
Bluntnose Shiner			21.6 (1)	1.9 (5)						
Emerald Shiner							--	11.5 (2)		
Common Carp							13.4 (2)	--		
Redhorse									9.6 (2)	--
White Sucker									9.6 (3)	--
Black Bullhead					26 (2)	4.7 (6)			60.5 (1)	6.2 (5)
Yellow Bullhead					2 (6)	2.3 (8)	--	3.0 (4)		
Channel Catfish	0.3 (5)	7.9 (2)					--	75.3 (1)		
Chinook Salmon	--	27.5 (1)								
Rainbow Trout	--	6.9 (3)								
Northern Pike									5.8 (4)	--
Walleye					--	34.8 (1)	11.3 (5)	--	--	10.8 (4)
Yellow Perch					8 (4)	15.6 (3)			5.2 (5)	11.0 (6)

TABLE 3-8 (page 2 of 2)
RELATIVE ABUNDANCE OF DOMINANT SPECIES COLLECTED IN IMPOUNDMENTS COMPARED TO ENTRAINED FISH AT MISCELLANEOUS PROJECTS IN MICHIGAN AND WISCONSIN

Species	Buchanan		Constantine		Crowley		Centralia		White Rapids	
	Imp.* (%)	Ent. (%)	Imp. (%)	Ent. (%)	Imp. (%)	Ent. (%)	Imp. (%)	Ent. (%)	Imp. (%)	Ent. (%)
Blackside Darter					--	4.8 (5)				
Log Perch	1.6 (4)	4.6 (9)	10.2 (4)	6.0 (2)	--	17.9 (2)				
Bluegill			15.5 (2)	3.5 (3)	8 (4)	--	--	4.2 (3)	--	13.7 (2)
Pumpkinseed					39 (1)					
Rock Bass					1 (7)	--	27.9 (1)			
Black Crappie					17 (3)	5.7 (4)	12.9 (4)	1.9 (5)	--	11.3 (3)
Smallmouth Bass							13.2 (3)	--		

*   Relative abundance of entrained fish at all sites determined by partial flow tailrace netting.

Note: Only dominant species included; dashes indicate incidental catch; numbers in parenthesis indicate species rank.   Impoundment populations sampled by electrofishing, fyke net, gill net, seine, and trap net.

TABLE 3-9

RELATIVE ABUNDANCE OF DOMINANT SPECIES COLLECTED IN IMPOUNDMENTS COMPARED TO ENTRAINED FISH AT MISCELLANEOUS PROJECTS IN OHIO AND GEORGIA

Species	King Mill			Greenup Lock & Dam	
	Imp. (%) 1984	Imp. (%) 1990	Ent. (%)[1] (1990)	Imp. (%)	Ent. (%)[2]
Threadfin Shad	--	--	35.4 (1)		
Blueback Herring	--	--	9.1 (3)		
Gizzard Shad	--	--	5.4 (5)	58 (1)	94.0 (1)
Emerald Shiner	--	--	--	6 (3)	
Spottail Shiner	--	--	12.8 (2)		
Golden Shiner	11.7 (4)	5.7 (5)	1.3 (14)		
Common Carp				3 (4)	--
River Carpsucker				3 (4)	--
Brown Bullhead	1.1 (7)	10.2 (3)	--		
Chain Pickerel	4.1 (5)	5.7 (5)	--		
Pirate Perch	--	--	4.9 (6)		
Yellow Perch	14.4 (2)	1.1 (8)	2.7 (7)		
Sauger				3 (4)	--
Freshwater Drum				3 (4)	5.0 (2)
Bluegill	22.0 (1)	34.1 (1)	7.9 (4)	10 (2)	--
Redear Sunfish	1.9 (6)	12.5 (2)	--		
Redbreast Sunfish	14.4 (2)	3.4 (7)	1.5 (12)		
Pumpkinseed	--	6.8 (4)	--		
Largemouth Bass				3 (4)	--

(1) Relative abundance of entrained fish determined by partial-flow tailrace netting.

(2) Relative abundance of entrained fish determined by partial-flow turbine gallery netting.

Note: Only dominant species included; dashes indicate incidental catch; numbers in parenthesis indicate species rank. Impoundment populations sampled by electrofishing, fyke net, gill net, seine, and trap net. Relative abundance of entrained fish at all sites on Au Sable River determined by partial flow tailrace netting.

TABLE 3-19
POPULATION ESTIMATES OF TARGET SPECIES COMPARED
TO ANNUAL ENTRAINMENT OF THOSE SPECIES

	Crowley				Rothschild				Wisconsin River Division				Centralia				Buzzards Roost			
	Impoundment		Entrained		Impoundment		Entrained		Impoundment		Entrained		Impoundment		Entrained		Impoundment		Entrained	
	Total No.	No./Acre	Total No.	Relative Rank	Total No.	No./Acre	Total No.	Relative Rank	Total No.	No./Acre	Total No.	Relative Rank	Total No.	No./Acre	Total No.	Relative Rank	Total No.	No./Acre	Total No.	Relative Rank
	154 (11-35")	0.4	0	--	5,560	3.5	111	(low)					4,058 (>13")	16.2	872	17	153,600,000	13,470	21,558,941	1
	12 (28-47")	<0.1	9	37																
	8,004 (3-26")	19	23,311	1	1,567 (>12")	1.0	7,525	6	3,685 (>8")	15.3	3,833	12	955 (>5")	3.8	3,020	8				
				11					10,571 (>2")	44.0	179,515	2								
									12,701 (>3")	52.9	8,351	7								
s									13,553 (>4")	56.5	23,762	5	1,184 (>4")	4.7	1,680	11				

TABLE 3.10
POPULATION ESTIMATES OF TARGET SPECIES COMPARED TO ANNUAL ENTRAINMENT OF THOSE SPECIES

	Crowley				Rothschild				Wisconsin River Division				Centralia				Buzzards Roost			
	Impoundment		Entrained		Impoundment		Entrained		Impoundment		Entrained		Impoundment		Entrained		Impoundment		Entrained	
	Total No.	No./Acre	Total No.	Relative Rank	Total No.	No./Acre	Total No.	Relative Rank	Total No.	No./Acre	Total No.	Relative Rank	Total No.	No./Acre	Total No	Relative Rank	Total No.	No./Acre	Total No.	Relative Rank
	154 (11-35")	0.4	0	--	5,560	3.5	111	(low)									153,600,000	13,470	21,558,941	1
	12 (28-47")	<0.1	9	37									4,058 (>13")	16.2	872	17				
	8,004 (3-26")	19	23,311	1	1,567 (>12")	1.0	7,525	6	3,685 (>8")	15.3	3,833	12								
				11					10,571 (>2")	44.0	179,515	2	955 (>5")	3.8	3,020	8				
									12,701 (>3")	52.9	8,351	7								
									13,553 (>4")	56.5	23,762	5	1,184 (>4")	4.7	1,680	11				

Annual entrainment of smallmouth bass at Wisconsin River Division (23,762 individuals; average size: 1.5 inches) is relatively high compared to the relatively low rate at Centralia (1,680 individuals). The density of smallmouth in the Wisconsin River Division impoundment, 56.5/acre, is the fifth highest of the 12 reported values in both natural and hydropower waterbodies in Wisconsin, as compared to the density of smallmouth bass at Centralia (4.7/acre) which ranked eleventh (Weyerhaeuser et al., 1993).

The density of black crappie in the Wisconsin River Division impoundment is roughly in the mid-range of the reported values for Wisconsin (Weyerhaeuser et al., 1993) and the relative abundance of entrained black crappie ranked seventh at this site (a moderate level relative to the other entrained species).

The remaining population estimate data can be compared to the associated entrainment values, but the usefulness of such comparisons given the previous discussion, is limited. There are no available data for making intersite comparisons of common carp, bluegill, or threadfin shad.

3.4 Summary of Entrainment Protective Measure Questionnaire Results

We sent the questionnaire to applicants for the 157 sites scheduled for license renewal in 1993. We received responses on 64 sites. No studies or protective were recommended by resource agencies at 31 of the sites. We received cost information on entrainment and turbine mortality studies and/or protective measures for 35 sites, including two not included in the original 157. We deleted information

for two sites because of ambiguous responses.

Cost information approximates actual costs associated with a study or protective measure. Conceptual costs (those expected to be incurred in the future) are not as reliable as actual costs, and the year when the cost was incurred or estimated introduces additional variability to the reported values. The nature of the affected resource and degree of resource agency intervention also influence entrainment-related costs. Site-specific conditions strongly influence costs of studies and protective measures.

3.4.1 Summary of Cost Information on Entrainment and Turbine Mortality Studies

We received cost figures for entrainment and turbine mortality studies for 12 sites (Table 3-11). We included only cost information from field studies. We obtained the approximate cost to conduct netting studies at Spartan Mills from material in the study report, however, not in response to the questionnaire. We supplemented this information with three study costs presented in Francfort et al. (1994). Costs reflect studies conducted between 1989 and 1992, with one exception (at Leaburg studies were conducted in 1981 and 1982).

Netting entrainment studies were generally two to four times more costly than hydroacoustic studies. Based on six studies, the mean cost to conduct hydroacoustic studies was $77,820 (range: $50,400-$105,000). All hydroacoustic studies but one (Little Falls on the Mohawk River) were supplemented by netting to obtain species and size information. Based on seven studies, the mean cost to conduct

TABLE 3-11
ENTRAINMENT AND TURBINE MORTALITY STUDY COST SUMMARY

Site (State)	Capacity		Years of Study	Study Cost		
	Hydraulic (cfs)	Electrical (MW)		Hydroacoustic	Netting	Turbine Mortality
Centralia (WI)	3640	3.2	1991-92	$94,093	$393,042	$2,100
Wisconsin River Division (WI)	5120	1.8	1991-92	105,000	210,000	(1)
Rothschild (WI)	3300	3.64	1991-92	(2)	310,000	10,000
Brule (WI)	1377	5.3	1990-92	68,000	218,000	(1)
White Rapids (WI)	5188	8	1990-92	68,000	218,000	70,000
Chalk Hill (WI)	3500	7.8	1992	(3)	(3)	70,000
Buchanan (MI)	3798	4.1	1991-92	(3)	442,000(4)	(1)
Station 26 (NY)	1800	3	1989-90	50,400	(3)	90,700 (5)
Station 5 (NY)	5000	38.25	(1995)	(3)	(3)	139,000 (5)
Station 2 (NY)	1400	6.5	(1995)	(3)	(3)	90,700 (5)
Glen Falls (NY)	--	12.09	1991	(3)	(3)	96,000
Little Falls (NY)	--	13.6	1989-90	81,430 (4)	(3)	(3)
Lowell (MA)	6450	15	1990-92	(3)	(3)	386,600 (4)
Spartan Mills (GA)	--	2.05	1991-92	(3)	120,000	(1)
Leaburg (OR)	2175	13.5	1981-82	(3)	--	51,000 (6)
Range of Costs				$50,400 - $105,000	$120,000 - $442,000	$2,100- $386,600
Mean Cost				$77,820	$273,006	$100,610

(1)   Turbine mortality study costs included in netting costs.
(2)   Studies completed but costs not reported.
(3)   Studies not done.
(4)   Source: Francfort et al. 1994; costs presented as 1993 dollars.
(5)   Projected cost of future studies.
(6)   Escalated to 1992 costs using ENR cost index.

Note: Respondents for three projects estimated that internal utility costs for managing studies and interacting with agencies was approximately $10,000 per year. Consumers Power indicated that they spent $1.75 million on entrainment (hydroacoustic supported by netting) and turbine survival studies at 11 plants (mean cost:$159,091).

entrainment studies by netting was $273,006 (range: $120,000-$442,000) and generally involved no more than six sampling days per month. Field work for all studies lasted about 1 year. Cost estimates for four of the seven netting studies are for studies done in conjunction with hydroacoustics. Conclusions based on costs from only five hydroacoustic studies and seven netting studies should be considered tentative.

Although hydroacoustic studies may be less costly, they often are less acceptable to agencies (e.g., resource agencies considered the two most expensive hydroacoustic studies invalid because of high ambient noise). Agencies also dismissed results from a hydroacoustic study at Rothschild (the cost of which was not provided). Agencies considered hydroacoustically derived entrainment estimates at White Rapids and Brule to be less accurate than those derived from netting studies.

Costs associated with turbine mortality studies are variable, ranging from $2,100 to $386,600. The least expensive studies are those conducted as a component of entrainment netting studies such as at Centralia and Rothschild because almost all equipment for testing is already in place. Incremental costs of turbine mortality studies at these two sites were estimated to be $2,100 and $10,000, respectively. Similar turbine mortality studies at three other sites were not readily separated from the cost of the netting studies.

Turbine mortality also can be assessed by marking fish upstream of a powerplant and recapturing or counting them at a downstream location, a technique that is especially effective for outmigrating anadromous fish. The Leaburg Project in Oregon studied salmon smolts during 1981 and 1982, which cost an estimated $40,000 at that time (nearly $51,000 in 1992 dollars). Several sites have used a promising new approach to assessing turbine mortality using balloon-tags that inflate after the fish passes through the turbine. Costs of balloon-tag studies from three sites (White Rapids, Chalk Hill, and Glen Falls) ranged from $70,000 to $90,700. Turbine mortality study costs for three more sites, ranging from $90,700 to $139,000, are conceptual and apply to unspecified techniques that applicants expect to implement in 1995.

The overall combined cost of conducting entrainment and turbine mortality studies at each site ranged from approximately $51,000 to $489,235. Electrical capacity of projects included in this assessment ranged from 1.8 to 38.2 MW. The capacity of all but five single-development projects ranged from 1 to < 10 MW. Sale et al. (1991) reported study costs associated with "downstream fish passage" for projects within this capacity range. Study costs of the 11 respondents to their questionnaire ranged from $5,657 to $281,428 with an average cost of $80,047. Average total cost of studies at the 10 sites within this capacity range reported herein (Table 3-11) is $263,003. This considerably higher cost may reflect an increase in cost of more recently conducted entrainment and turbine mortality studies or a difference in the nature of study costs provided by respondents to the two questionnaires (e.g., the DOE report includes assessment of bypass efficiency and survival).

3.4.2 Summary of Cost Information on Recommended Entrainment Protective Measures

Costs of entrainment protective measures depend on site-specific conditions.

For example, the amount of civil engineering needed to install a device has a dramatic influence on its cost. The size of the river and flow characteristics at the project intake substantially influence the options for protective devices and the annual costs of operation, maintenance, and lost generation.

Management objectives for protective devices also have important cost implications. If the goal is simply to exclude fish from turbine passage, then a barrier device may suffice. If downstream passage of fish also is a goal, the barrier device must incorporate a system to safely bypass fish to a downstream location.

Sale et al. (1991) and EPRI (1986, 1994a, and 1994b) provide discussions of types of entrainment protective measures recently installed at sites. Information on cost and effectiveness of entrainment protective measures was recently compiled by the Idaho National Engineering Laboratory (INEL) under contract with the U.S. Department of Energy (Francfort et al., 1994).

Respondents to the questionnaire provided estimates of the constructed cost of protective measures for eight sites, and we supplemented these data with data from seven more sites described in Francfort et al. (1994). Conceptual costs for 20 sites were provided in response to our questionnaire and supplemented by cost data for 5 additional sites obtained from study reports. Section 4.2 presents the range of construction costs for all major categories of fish protective systems drawing from SWEC's past and ongoing work in fish protective. Cost data summarized below represent only the 40 sites where information was obtained from questionnaire respondents, study reports, or Francfort et

al. (1994). All sites with summarized data are conventional hydroelectric plants (i.e., data were not available for pumped storage projects).

Seven of the projects with installed protective measures are located in the northeast and reflect the management objective of protecting Atlantic salmon and/or clupeids from entrainment. A 1-inch trashrack was installed at the Millinocket Pumping Station to prevent landlocked Atlantic salmon from being entrained at a non-power producing facility, hence a fish bypass was not included. The other six sites in the northeast incorporated fish bypass systems into protective measures. Design and construction costs for these seven projects ranged from $4,700 to $130,140.

Another way of looking at costs of protective measures is to consider the cost per hydraulic capacity of the plant. This is a commonly used pricing index, because the cost of constructing most protective devices is closely related to the flow rate of the intake. The cost/cfs for design and construction of protective measures for the five projects in the northeast for which hydraulic capacity was available ranged from $9/cfs to $352/cfs, with the lowest value associated with the greatest hydraulic capacity. Costs presented above are substantially lower than those typically incurred for protective of anadromous species in the Pacific Northwest and reflected in the $808/cfs to $1,480/cfs shown in Table 3-12.

One questionnaire response provided cost information for screening systems designed primarily to protect anadromous salmonids in the Pacific Northwest, including the actual cost for one constructed facility and conceptual costs for a second facility. Constructed costs were supplied for

TABLE 3-12 (page 1 of 2)

ACTUAL COSTS ASSOCIATED WITH INSTALLATION OF PROTECTIVE MEASURES DESIGNED TO MINIMIZE ENTRAINMENT

(State)	Species of Concern	Plant Capacity Hydraulic (cfs)	Plant Capacity Electrical (MW)	Year(s) Cost Incurred	Description of Protective Measure	Design Costs	Construction Costs ($)	Construction & Design Costs/cfs ($)	Annual O&M Costs ($)	Annual Lost Generation Costs ($)	Effectiveness Study Costs ($)
cket ig (ME)	Atlantic salmon (landlocked)	250	None	1988-89	1-inch trashrack	(1)	88,000	352	?	N/A	6,000 (100% effective for salmon)
de in	Resident and anadromous salmonids	115	0.4	1986-87	Cylindrical wedgewire screens with air backflush	14,200(3)	78,700	808	3000	N/A	5,000(conducted over 5 years); drought has precluded use by anadromous salmonids.
ms	Atlantic salmon (landlocked)	150	0.6	1983	Angled 1-inch bar rack and bypass sluice	--	4,700	31	240	1,944	--
stone	Resident species	66	0.9	1992-93	Fish-stop grate	1,500	6,000	114	--	--	--
yd	Anadromous salmonids	500	1.2	1985-86	Angled trash rack; inclined 0.5-inch fish screen; bypass weir	71,110	621,600	1385	20,000	N/A	--
ter (ME)	Atlantic salmon and clupeids	1700	1.95	1992-93	Fish bypass weir with lighting and 1-inch trashrack	(1)	58,500	34	?	?	--
ls (ME)	Atlantic salmon and clupeids	3207	3.5	1990	Fish bypass system	5,000	33,000	12	?	?	--
VT	Resident species	624	3.6	1990-91	265-ft long barrier net	10,000	25,000	56	2-3000	--	200,000 (2-year EPRI co-funded study) (85-100% effective, less effective for fish <100mm)
d (ME)	Atlantic salmon and clupeids	5630	6.4	1992-93	Fish bypass system	5,000	45,000	9	1,100	26,200	--
rth (ME)	Atlantic salmon and clupeids	--	8.9	1989	Fish bypass system, with a 10-ft wide weir	(1)	98,000	--	?	17,280	--
g (OR)	Anadromous salmonids	2175	13.5	1982-83	Patented V screen in power canal with wedgewire screening and diversion system	200,000 (253,715)(2)	1,440,000 (1,826,750)(2) plus $1,139,297 for improvements over 10 years	1,480	12,500	300,000	70,000/yr (1993)(90-98.6% effective in protecting fry when screen debris buildup controlled)
Falls	Anadromous blueback herring	--	13.6	1989-90	0.5-inch mesh screens/0.5-inch drilled plate with fish bypass system	(1)	130,140	--	6000	--	261,250 (1992) (licensee estimates fewer than 1% of herring in area were entrained. Study results subjective.)
sullivan	Anadromous salmonids	23,810 (average site flow)	16.6	1980	Eicher screen & guidance system	(1)	408,413 (1 of 13 penstocks)	--	12,000	63,000	60,000/yr (bypass efficiency: 77-95%)

TABLE 3-11 (page 2 of 2)

Species of Concern	Plant Capacity		Year(s) Cost Incurred	Description of Protective Measure	Design Costs	Construction Costs ($)	Construction & Design Costs/csf ($)	Annual O&M Costs ($)	Annual Lost Generation Costs ($)	Effectiveness Study Costs ($)
	Hydraulic (cfs)	Electrical (MW)								
Resident trout	710	24	1989-93	Inclined wedgewire screens with air backflush	27,820	996,720	1,443	5,000	--	17,120 (system meets agency guidelines)
Anadromous salmonids	48,950 (average site flow)	810	1992-93	19 submerged traveling screens and 18 vertical barrier screens	(1)	4,996,900	--	274,800	--	244,700 (1992) (total fish guidance efficiency ranged from 35% for subyearling chinook salmon to 74% for steelhead)

sign costs not separated from construction costs.
unce: Francfort et al. 1994; costs reported as 1993 dollars.
:ludes licensing costs.
:alated to 1992 costs using ENR cost index.

the Leaburg Project, where a patented V-configured wedgewire screening and bypass system was installed in the power canal in 1983. Approximate cost for the initial design and construction of this facility, escalated to 1992 dollars, was $2,080,465. Additional improvements to the system were made to conform to resource agency recommendations during the 10 years that this system has operated and total $1,139,297. Therefore, the total cost of the facility as it is presently operating is $3,219,762 ($1,480/cfs).

The Leaburg Project dramatically illustrates that the initial design and construction costs for protective measures are frequently less than the total costs of making the device fully functional. Additional capital costs may be incurred as a result of agency-recommended effectiveness studies that provide a basis for evaluation of performance goals and subsequent system modifications. The most recent (1993) annual cost associated with evaluating effectiveness of the Leaburg system was $70,000. At the Sullivan Project annual study costs are estimated to be $60,000. The approximate average annual operation and maintenance costs ($12,000 to $12,500) and lost generation costs ($63,000 to $300,000) also represent substantial costs associated with the protective measures at these projects.

Exclusion of resident species was the goal of three protective systems for which costs were provided: Twin Falls, Yellowstone, and Pine. The estimated cost of installing a "fish-stop grate" at the Yellowstone Project and a 265-foot-long barrier net at the Pine Project was $7,500 ($114/cfs) and $35,000 ($56/cfs), respectively. The installation at the Pine Project is representative of the costs at a small project ideally suited to this technology. Installations at more complex projects, such as Brule and White Rapids (see Table 3-13), can be considerably more costly and illustrate the site-specific nature of the cost to install protective measures. A major cost associated with barrier nets is often operation and maintenance. O&M costs were estimated at $2,000 to $3,000 per year at Pine including replacement net costs, but may be substantially higher at sites with substantial debris loading.

Installation costs associated with the inclined wedgewire screens at Twin Falls were substantially higher than Yellowstone and Pine. The installation cost of $1,024,540 ($1,443/cfs) rivals that of other Pacific Northwest facilities designed to protect anadromous salmonids. The unusually high cost is largely influenced by underground construction required at this site. Although costs at this site could be considered unique, this case underscores the site-specific nature of protective measure costs.

Most respondents provided information on the conceptual cost of constructing protective measures in the future, since the questionnaire was sent to applicants of projects scheduled to be relicensed by the end of 1993. In some cases, the installation of protective measures was agreed to by the applicants and construction scheduled for completion within 2 or 3 years of license issuance (Table 3-13). Costs associated with these projects may be more representative than other conceptual costs presented for projects at which the timing and/or need for the protective measure has not been clearly established.

(this page intentionally left blank)

TABLE 5-13

CONCEPTUAL COSTS ASSOCIATED WITH INSTALLATION OF PROTECTIVE MEASURES DESIGNED TO MINIMIZE ENTRAINMENT

Site	State	Species of Concern	Plant Capacity Hydraulic (cfs)	Plant Capacity Electrical (MW)	Year Costs[1] Expected	Description of Protective Measure	Design Costs ($)	Construction Costs ($)	Construction + Design Costs/cfs ($)	Annual O&M Costs ($)	Annual Lost Generation Costs ($)	Effectiveness Study Costs ($)
Pierce Mills	VT	Atl Salmon	200	0.3	1995	1 inch trashrack overlay with bypass	2,000[2]	30,000	160	-	-	-
Station 160	NY	Resident Species	340	0.3	1995	1 inch trashrack with bypass	-	222,000	653	47,374	3,049	-
Arnold Falls	VT	Atl Salmon	260	0.4	1995	1 inch trashrack with bypass	2,000[2]	35,000	142	-	-	-
Taftsville	VT	Atl Salmon	370	0.5	1995	1 inch trashrack with bypass	2,000[2]	46,000	130	-	-	-
Gage	VT	Atl Salmon	700	0.7	1995	1 inch trashrack overlay with bypass	2,000[2]	67,500	99	-	-	-
Passumpsic	VT	Atl Salmon	460	0.7	1995	1 inch trashrack overlay with bypass	2,000[2]	32,000	74	-	-	-
Fort Halifax	ME	Atl Salmon, clupeids	1,700	1.5	1993	1 inch trashrack with bypass	20,000[2]	220,000	141	10,000	?	-
North Gorham	ME	Resident Species, Atl Salmon	950	2.3	?(1994)	Bypass	-	342,000	360	-	198,000 [3]	-
Station 26	NY	Resident Species	1,800	3.0	1995	1 inch trashrack with bypass	-	790,000	439	94,748	11,100	-
Beaver Falls[4]	PA	Clupeids, Resident Species	4,400	5.0	?(1992)	1 inch trashrack (2600 square feet)	-	456,525	104	40,000	?	-
						Sound Deterrent	-	178,000	40	8,500	-	-
						Electric Screen Diversion	-	72,000	16	8,000	-	-
						Traveling Screen	-	472,050	107	15,000	?	-
Brule	WI	Resident Species	1377	5.3	1995	Barrier Net (190 ft)	5,000[2]	72,000	56	-	-	70,000
Watertown	NY	Resident Species	6,000	5.4	1995	1 inch trashrack with bypass	-	300,000	50	?	28,000	-
Station 2	NY	Resident Species	1,400	6.5	1995	1 inch trashrack with bypass	-	483,000	61	47,000	38,500	-
Bonny Eagle	ME	Atl Salmon, Clupeids	4,800	7.2	1995	Bypass	-	200,000	42	10,000	-	200,000 (over 3 years)
Essex 19	VT	Atl Salmon	2,000	7.2	1995	1 inch trashrack overlay with bypass	-	250,000	125	-	-	-
Chalk Hill	WI	Resident Species	3,500	7.8	?(1989)	1 inch trashrack	20,000[2]	4,300,000 (+275,000 lost generation)	1,313 (includes lost generation during construction)	-	-	100,000

TABLE 3-13

CONCEPTUAL COSTS ASSOCIATED WITH INSTALLATION OF PROTECTIVE MEASURES DESIGNED TO MINIMIZE ENTRAINMENT

Site	State	Species of Concern	Plant Capacity Hydraulic (cfs)	Plant Capacity Electrical (MW)	Year Cost(f) Expected	Description of Protective Measure	Design Costs ($)	Construction Costs ($)	Construction + Design Costs/cfs ($)	Annual O&M Costs ($)	Annual Lost Generation Costs ($)	Effectiveness Study Costs ($)
Waterville	OR	Anadromous Salmonids	>2,175	8.0	1995	Patented V-Screen in Power Canal with Wedge Wire Screening and Diversion System	368,500[2]	7,100,000	-3,434	12,500	?	?
White Rapids[4]	WI	Resident Species	5,188	8.0	?	Barrier Net (Simplified)	20,000[2]	90,000	21	90,000		100,000
						Barrier with Supports (450 ft Long)		1,370,000	264			
						Barrier Net (325 ft long) with spillway separation wall		3,460,000	667	60,000	?	
						1 inch trashrack (160 ft long)		4,260,000 (+325,000 lost generation)	884 (Includes lost generation during construction)			
Weston	ME	Atl Salmon, Clupeids	5,960	12.0	2001	Bypass	-	300,000	50	10,000	-	-
Glen Falls	NY	Resident Species	?	12.1	~1995	Not Yet Determined	270,000	1,800,000	-	?	?	-
	SC	Clupeids, Resident Species										
Buzzards Roost[4]			4,000	15.0	?(1992)	1 inch trashrack (1120 ft long)	-	10,764,587	2,691	?	?	-
Skelton	ME	Atl Salmon, Clupeids	3,800	16.8	1996	Bypass	-	200,000	53	-	-	-
Station 5	NY	Resident Species	5,000	38.3	1995	1 inch trashrack with bypass	-	1,529,000	306	180,000	142,000	-
Hawks Nest[4]	WV	Clupeids, Resident Species	10,000	102.0[5]	?(1990)	8-traveling screens (47 ft deep and 110 ft long)	-	11,000,000	1,100	?	?	-
Glen Ferris[4]	WV											
-W. Powerhouse		Resident Species	930		?(1990)	3 traveling screens (14 ft deep and 83 ft long)	-	1,650,000	1,774	?	?	-
-E. Powerhouse		Resident Species	2,400		?(1990)	6 traveling screens (15 ft deep and 61 ft long)	-	7,250,000	3,021	?	?	-

nentation date is unknown, the year dollar values estimated is presented in parenthesis
have already been incurred (between 1989 and 1993)
generation for the term of the license
osts obtained from entrainment study reports
pacity of Hawks Nest and Glen Ferris developments is combined

Because applicants/licensees generally only install up-front (i.e., without entrainment studies) protective measures for resident fish when they are inexpensive, "actual" costs may not be representative of typical sites.

Table 3-13 presents conceptual costs for protective measures at 25 sites. All but one of the 17 northeast sites include fish bypass systems and a specified component of these systems is often an angled 1-inch trashrack. It is likely that a 1-inch trashrack is also a component at some of the sites where it is not specified. One-inch trashrack costs are also provided for five of the eight remaining sites outside of the northeast. The most expensive protective measures based on total conceptual cost are the 110-foot-long, 47-foot-deep traveling screen system at Hawks Nest ($11,000,000) and a 1,120-foot-long, 1-inch trashrack system proposed for Buzzard's Roost ($10,764,587). The most expensive protective measures from a cost/cfs perspective are the Walterville V-configured wedgewire screen system ($3,434/cfs) and the 61-foot-long, 15-foot-deep traveling screen system at the east powerhouse of the Glen Ferris Project ($3,021/cfs). The least expensive protective measure based on total cost is a $32,000 1-inch trashrack overlay with a bypass system proposed for the Pierce Mills Project in Vermont.

Actual costs to design and install protective measures for projects with a capacity of less than 1 MW ranged from $4,700 to $92,900 (Table 3-14) and conceptual costs ranged from $32,000 to $222,000 (Table 3-15). These costs are generally higher than the range of $416 to $122,060 for 12 projects reported in Sale et al. (1991). Protective measures reported by Sale include projects with angled trashracks

(with and without bypass systems), velocity limits, and wedgewire screening systems.

Most projects for which actual and conceptual costs for protective measures were provided have a capacity of from 1 to less than 10 MW. Actual capital costs for protective measures for projects of this size ranged from $35,000 to $692,710 (Table 3-14). Conceptual capital costs for protective measures ranged from $72,000 to $7,468,500 (Table 3-15). These costs are generally comparable to costs reported by Sale et al. (1991) for developments of the same capacity, which ranged from $0 (reflecting a plant that modified its turbine sequencing to protect fish) to $2,374,268 (reflecting a plant that uses angled trashracks and a velocity limit on intake screens to protect anadromous and resident juvenile fish). Estimated actual O&M costs associated with the facilities represented by the present study ranged from $1,100 to $20,000 (capacity range: 1 to <10 MW) and conceptual O&M costs ranged from $8,000 to $94,748. Sale et al. (1991) reported O&M costs of $0 to $43,169 for projects of similar capacity.

Actual and conceptual capital costs for plants with a capacity of 10 to 50 MW ranged from $200,000 to $11,000,000 and are generally higher than the range for projects with the same capacity reported by Sale et al. (1991), $92,996 to $2,807,381.

Reported costs for specific protective measures are variable (Table 3-16) and primarily associated with the costs of 1-inch trashracks. In part, this may be due to differences in the size and configuration of the intakes at various projects. In addition, different orientation (and therefore size) of trashracks may be necessary to reduce effective intake velocities experienced by fish to minimize entrainment. Some of the

	Capacity Category			
Cost Type	<1 MW	1 - <10 MW	10 - <50 MW	>50 MW
Capital Costs (Design and Construct)				
Total				
resident fish sites	$4,700 - 92,900 (4)	$35,000 (1)	1,024,540(1)	-- (0)
anadromous fish sites	-- (0)	$38,000 - 692,710 (5)	$130,140-3,219,762(3)	4,996,900 (1)
Cost/cfs				
resident fish sites	$31-808 (4)	$56 (1)	$1,443 (1)	-- (0)
anadromous fish sites	-- (0)	$9 - 1385 (4)	$1,480 (1)	-- (0)
Annual Operation and Maintenance Costs				
resident fish sites	$240 - 3000 (2)	$2,000 - 3,000 (1)	$5,000 (1)	-- (0)
anadromous fish sites	-- (0)	$1,100 - 20,000 (2)	$6,000 - 12,500 (3)	$274,800 (1)
Annual Lost Generation Costs				
resident fish sites	$1944 (1)	-- (0)	-- (0)	-- (0)
anadromous fish sites	-- (0)	$17,280 - 26,200 (2)	$63,000 - 300,000 (2)	-- (0)
Effectiveness Evaluation Costs				
Annual				
resident fish sites	$1000 (1)	-- (0)	-- (0)	-- (0)
anadromous fish sites	-- (0)	-- (0)	$60,000 - 70,000 (2)	-- (0)
Total				
resident fish sites	$6,000 (1)	$200,000 (1)	$17,120 (1)	-- (0)
anadromous fish sites	-- (0)	-- (0)	$261,250 (1)	244,700 (1)

TABLE 3-14

SUMMARY OF ACTUAL COSTS ASSOCIATED WITH INSTALLATION OF ENTRAINMENT PROTECTIVE MEASURES

Note: Numbers in parenthesis represent number of sites included in the range.

TABLE 3-15
SUMMARY OF CONCEPTUAL COSTS ASSOCIATED WITH
INSTALLATION OF ENTRAINMENT PROTECTIVE MEASURES

Cost Type	Capacity Category		
	< 1 MW	1- < 10 MW	10- < 50 MW
Capital Costs (Design and Construct)			
Total			
resident fish sites	$222,000 (1)	$72,000 - 4,595,000 (13)	$1,528,000-10,764,587 (6)
anadromous fish sites	$32,500 - 69,500 (5)	$200,000 - 7,468,500 (5)	$200,000 - 300,000 (2)
Cost/cfs			
resident fish sites	$653 (1)	$16 - 1,313 (12)	$306 - 3,021 (5)
anadromous fish sites	$74 - 160 (5)	$42 - 3,434 (5)	$50 - 53 (2)
Annual Operation and Maintenance Costs			
resident fish sites	$47,374 (1)	$8,000 - 94,748 (8)	$180,000 (1)
anadromous fish sites	-- (0)	$10,000 - 12,500 (3)	$10,000 (1)
Annual Lost Generation Costs			
resident fish sites	$3,049 (1)	$11,100 - 38,500 (3)*	$142,000 (1)
anadromous fish sites	-- (0)	-- (0)	-- (0)
Effectiveness Evaluation Costs			
Annual			
resident fish sites	-- (0)	-- (0)	-- (0)
anadromous fish sites	-- (0)	-- (0)	-- (0)
Total			
resident fish sites	-- (0)	$70,000 - 100,000 (3)	-- (0)
anadromous fish sites	-- (0)	$200,000 (1)	-- (0)

*   One additional respondent presented lost generation costs for the term of the license, which was $198,000.

Note: Costs presented by respondents were either escalated to year when costs scheduled to occur or, if year of construction unknown, to the year when the estimate was made. Dollar values ranged from 1989 to 1995 and, because costs are conceptual, no attempt was made to escalate these estimates. Numbers in parenthesis represent number of sites included in the range.

TABLE 3-16
RANGE OF DESIGN AND CONSTRUCTION COSTS ASSOCIATED
WITH SPECIFIC ENTRAINMENT PROTECTIVE MEASURES

Item	Actual Cost		Conceptual Cost	
	Total	Cost/cfs	Total	Cost/cfs
One-inch Trashracks:				
Trashrack only	$88,000 (1)	$352 (1)	$456,525 - 10,764,587 (4)	$104 - 2,691 (4)
Trashrack Overlay with Bypass System	$130,140 (1)	--	$32,000 - 250,000 (4)	$74 - 142 (4)
Trashrack with Bypass System	$4,700 - 58,000 (2)	$31 - 34 (2)	$37,000 - 1,529,000 (8)	$50 - 653 (8)
Fish Bypass System (may incorporate one-inch trashracks)	$38,000 - 98,000 (3)	$9 - 12 (2)	$200,000 - 342,000 (4)	$42 - 360 (4)
Angled trashrack, 0.5-in. inclined fish screen with bypass	$692,710 (1)	$1,385 (1)	--	--
Fish Stop Grate	$7,500 (1)	$114 (1)	--	--
Barrier Nets:				
Simplified	$35,000 (1)	$56 (1)	$77,000 - $110,000 (2)	$21 - 56 (2)
With Supports	--	--	$1,370,000 (1)	$264 (1)
With Spillway Separation Wall	--	--	$3,460,000 (1)	$667 (1)
V-configured Wedgewire Screen with Bypass System	$3,219,762 (1)	$1,480 (1)	$7,468,500 (1)	$3,434 (1)
Cylindrical Wedgewire Screen with Air Backflush	$92,900 (1)	$808 (1)	--	--
Inclined Wedgewire Screen with Air Backflush	$1,024,540 (1)	$1,443 (1)	--	--
Eicher Screen	$408,413 (1)	--	--	--
Traveling Screen	$4,996,900 (1)	--	$472,000 - $11,000,000* (4)	$107 - 3,021 (4)
Electric Screens	--	--	$72,000 (1)	$16 (1)
Sound Deterrent System	--	--	$178,000 (1)	$40 (1)

*   Costs for four developments at two projects.

Note: Numbers in parenthesis represent number of sites included in the range. Costs do not include lost generation during construction.

least and most expensive protective measures use 1-inch trashracks whether considered on a total cost or cost per cfs basis. Sale et al. (1991) also found little correlation between the cost and the specific protective measure employed. One project included in their database reported total capital costs of $3,238 for angled trashracks, velocity limit on intake screens, and fish bypass systems. In general, installing traveling screens seems to be the most expensive protective measure, with costs starting at approximately $0.5 million.

Construction costs for specific protective measures can be accurately estimated given sufficient design information on the device and adequate knowledge of site conditions. Lost generation related to bypass flows and head loss caused by screening systems also can be estimated, but less predictable are the future costs of O&M, effectiveness studies, and subsequent modifications that may be needed in response to these studies. Costs may range from virtually nothing to costs that exceed the initial capital costs of the protective measure. This uncertainty should be reduced as much as possible before deciding to implement specific measures. Conducting economic analyses of preferred options and establishing the potential for additional modifications by continuous interactions with resource agencies will help reduce uncertainty.

The questionnaire asked for information on the effectiveness of specific protective measures, but respondents provided very little information in this area. Section 4.2 presents information on effectiveness.

(this page intentionally left blank)

4.0 DISCUSSION

4.1 Extrapolation of Entrainment Data

Our statistical trend analyses (see Section 3.2.5) do not reveal consistent patterns to use for extrapolating entrainment results from one site to another site. Much of the variability in entrainment results between sites, however, may be caused by differences and biases in the sampling methodology, rather than by meaningful differences between sites. If study design and sampling methods are standardized (see Section 4.5), some statistically significant relationships may be identified in future entrainment studies.

Lack of consistent statistical significance does not necessarily indicate that it is inappropriate to use the results at one site to make decisions about protective measures at another site. Decisions on fish protection should be based on the level of impact, which cannot be determined from total entrainment values. Total entrainment values also do not account for the size and species composition of entrained fish.

Entrainment studies at a number of sites within a watershed may be used to extrapolate to other sites, especially sites in the same watershed. (Table 3-1 shows how such an extrapolation might be implemented). Using the entrainment rate adjusted for the hydraulic capacity of the plant (fish/hour/kcfs) probably is the most reasonable predictive value for extrapolation. For our analysis, we used the hydraulic capacity of the facility. When extrapolating results from one site to another, however, the best method is to use actual flow through the plant.

When more than one entrainment study was conducted on a river, the mean entrainment rate is also presented. This mean value sometimes does not accurately represent the site-specific entrainment rate at one site. For example, on the Au Sable River the entrainment rate at Five Channels is twice that of the mean value. On the Muskegon River, the entrainment rate at Hardy is one fifth of the mean value. Site-specific characteristics may account for these differences; e.g., the Five Channels impoundment is the shortest and narrowest of the six sites studied on the Au Sable River, and Hardy is the only site of the three studied on the Muskegon River with an intake tower that draws water from the surface, the bottom, or both. Accounting for such characteristics may reduce the variability of entrainment rates between sites and help to identify appropriate sites for extrapolation.

A decision to extrapolate entrainment data from one site to another should account for the relative value of the potential lost fishery. Because most entrained fish are the result of pulsed movements of young individuals, the actual loss to the fishery resource could be more similar among projects within the same basin than total entrainment rates would indicate.

Applying the mean entrainment rate to other sites in the same watershed may have some predictive value. The mean entrainment rate at Brule, located 2 miles upstream of the confluence of the Brule River with the Menominee River, was 3.5 fish/hour/kcfs, which is similar to the mean value of 2.6 fish/hour/kcfs for two sites on the Menominee River. Because of the small number of values available for comparison in this case, however, this similarity may not be representative.

A review of the entrainment rates in Table 3-1 clearly indicates that it may not be appropriate to extrapolate entrainment results when entrainment at one site is heavily dominated by clupeids and the other sites are not (e.g., the Buzzard's Roost site [entrainment rate: 623.0 fish/hour/kcfs] compared to the other Broad River watershed sites [entrainment rate: 4.1-10.4 fish/hour/kcfs]). It may be possible to extrapolate between sites if both are dominated by clupeids. Prior knowledge of the potentially affected fisheries resource is necessary before considering extrapolation.

Assessment of varied monthly entrainment rates for representative species, without accounting for project proximity (Section 3.2.6), indicates that it may be difficult to establish an action "trigger" (that rate at which protective measures at an unsampled site may be required) of entrainment rate for specific species. Monthly entrainment rates were extremely variable between sites, although there were some seasonal trends (e.g., low entrainment rates of smallmouth bass, walleye, and white sucker during the winter). Variable monthly entrainment rates between sites may not substantially affect the relative annual entrainment rate if the variable rates are caused by a seasonal shift in entrainment. In other cases, however, the monthly variability relative to other sites in the same basin is much greater than can reasonably be attributed to seasonal shifts (e.g., smallmouth bass at Wisconsin River Division; walleye at Foote and Hardy; and black crappie at Croton, White Rapids, Rothschild, and Ninety-nine Islands). At some sites, the entrainment rate for some species is substantially different than for others during specific times of the year. Such major variations translate into intersite differences in annual entrainment rates for

certain species that may not be attributable to an identifiable cause.

When considering extrapolation of entrainment results at sampled sites to unsampled sites there is a risk that a licensee/applicant could be required to install protective measures that are not really necessary, or that protective measures will not be recommended at sites where their installation is justified. This risk must be recognized when evaluating the appropriateness of extrapolation. The risks associated with extrapolation can, however, be minimized if entrainment studies at sampled sites are carefully designed and implemented using standardized procedures and/or the resource loss is of less value than the cost of protective measures (see Sections 4.4 and 4.5). Risks can be further reduced by confining extrapolation to sites within the same basin and with similar site characteristics (e.g., presence of clupeids, presence of upstream stocking programs, or similar site configuration).

4.2 Cost and Effectiveness of Protective Measures

Responses to our questionnaire provided little information on the effectiveness of protective measures, because few applicants had installed and evaluated measures. Many respondents indicated that protective measures were scheduled to be installed within 2 to 3 years after issuance of a new license. It will probably take an additional 1 to 2 years before the results of evaluation studies are available for most of these sites.

Because of the limited information gathered from the questionnaire, we supplemented this section with other sources available to SWEC from past and ongoing fish protection studies conducted for the

Electric Power Research Institute (EPRI), DOE (Francfort et al., 1994), and individual licensees/applicants.

The following sections summarize available information on the cost and effectiveness of commonly prescribed protective measures and of other technologies that are currently under development.

4.2.1 Low-Velocity Fish Screens

Low-velocity fish screens provide a sufficient amount of screen area to lower velocity approaching the screen and minimize potential impingement and injury. Most current designs set screens at an angle to the flow to direct fish towards downstream bypasses. Types of screening facilities most commonly considered include rotary drum screens; vertical traveling screens; and stationary screens equipped with debris removal apparatus such as traveling brushes, high-pressure backwash, or air-burst systems.

Low-velocity screening systems are the protective measure most readily accepted by fisheries agencies in the Pacific Northwest. Agencies there prefer to use well-proven technologies to protect valuable runs of salmon and/or steelhead trout. Many state agencies, as well as the regional office of the National Marine Fisheries Service, have developed design criteria for such screening and bypass facilities. Facilities usually are constructed to protect newly emergent fry with an approach velocity (perpendicular to the screen face) of 0.4 feet per second (fps). California recommends a maximum approach velocity of 0.33 fps.

Low-velocity screening systems are a relatively well-proven protective measure

for juvenile salmonids. Evaluation of 10 angled drum screen facilities in the Yakima River Basin (Hosey & Associates, 1990; Neitzel et al., 1990) showed that the proportion of bypassed fish with substantial scale loss or mortality usually is less than 1 or 2 percent. Potential losses from predation and/or escapement past the screen seals have not been as thoroughly evaluated. Predatory fish and/or birds may take some fish within the low-velocity area of the facility itself, and predation is a common problem at outfalls where bypassed fish are returned to the river (outfall predation is a potential problem for any bypass system [Francfort et al., 1994]). Poorly installed or worn screen seals also can allow fish to escape past the screens, particularly at rotary or vertical traveling screens. Evaluations to date have rarely demonstrated a recovery rate exceeding 90 percent of the fish released upstream of the facility. This may be due to nonmigratory behavior (residualism) of some test fish or to losses from predation and/or escapement past the screens.

Capital costs of constructing low-velocity screening systems generally range from $1,300 to $10,000 per cfs of plant capacity. This cost range is based on sites where the screening facility is located in a shallow power or irrigation canal and on sites in the Pacific Northwest where the primary objective is protection of juvenile and smolts of salmonid species. Construction costs probably would exceed this range in deep forebay applications due to the extensive civil works needed to support a large screening facility. Most designs cannot prevent damage from winter ice or severe debris loading, and maintenance costs can be substantial. Another drawback in constructing such a facility is that it usually requires a large area to be fenced off for public safety and to prevent vandalism, which affects public access and aesthetics.

4.2.2 High-Velocity Fish Screens

Several newer screen designs may provide equal or better protection at approach velocities well in excess of those at low-velocity screening systems. Designs include the fixed panel, "vee" design employed at the Leaburg Project in Oregon; the "Eicher Screen" designed for application in penstocks; and the "Modular Inclined Screen" under development by EPRI. All three designs use wedgewire or profile bar screen material, which provides a very smooth surface that minimizes injury or impingement.

Leaburg "Vee" Screen

The "vee" screen at the Leaburg Project was installed in 1983, and has subsequently been patented by the Eugene Water and Electric Board (EWEB). It has six vertical screen panels in a "triple-vee" configuration. The facility was designed with an average approach velocity (perpendicular to the screen) of 0.75 fps, and most evaluation testing has been conducted at approach velocities between 0.6 and 0.75 fps. After initial testing, a pressure backwash system for debris removal and adjustable baffles behind the screen were added to provide a more uniform flow distribution along the length of the screen panels. EWEB reports that, in recent tests, small salmon fry (35 to 40 mm) are protected from entrainment at a 98.6 percent rate at full canal flows when debris build-up on the screen is controlled (EWEB, 1993). Construction costs reported for the Leaburg screen, including modifications, are $1,480 per cfs (escalated to 1992 dollars). EWEB is designing a similar facility for their Walterville Project, with an estimated construction cost of $3,434 per cfs. These costs fall within the lower end of the range usually reported for low-velocity screening systems.

Eicher Screen

The Eicher Screen, designed for use in penstocks, provides effective fish diversion at approach velocities (perpendicular to the screen) in excess of 2 fps. The design has an inclined wedgewire screen mounted on a pivot shaft, which allows the screen to be tilted to flush debris. The design was initially developed for application at the Portland General Electric's Sullivan Hydroelectric Project on the Willamette River in Oregon, and it was patented by George Eicher. Despite poor hydraulic conditions imposed by the layout of the intake structure, evaluations in 1981 with salmon and steelhead smolts indicated that the screen has a diversion efficiency of at least 94.9 percent to 99.6 percent (Clark, 1981). Recent studies conducted with an improved sampling facility also demonstrated low injury rates, generally less than 3 percent even without accounting for pre-existing injuries (Clark and Cramer, 1993).

To fully evaluate the potential effectiveness of this screen design, EPRI funded evaluation studies during 1990 and 1991 of an Eicher Screen installed by James River II, Inc. in a 9-foot-diameter penstock at the Elwha Hydroelectric Project in Washington. The screen was installed in a straight penstock section, providing more uniform hydraulic conditions than existed in the irregularly shaped intake of the Sullivan Project.

Extensive evaluation demonstrated that the Eicher Screen at Elwha was highly effective in diverting steelhead trout, coho and chinook salmon smolts with minimal losses. Diversion efficiency exceeded 99 percent overall for all three species of smolts evaluated (EPRI, 1992a) at penstock velocities ranging from 4 to 7.8 fps. These test velocities equate to an average velocity perpendicular to the screen of 1.35 to 2.67 fps. The average passage survival (fish diverted live and surviving 96 hours following passage) ranged from 98.8 percent to 99.4 percent for the three species of smolts. A limited series of tests conducted with steelhead and coho fry indicated that passage survival exceeded 95 percent at penstock velocities of less than 7 fps. Debris tests conducted with all three species indicated that the potential for fish injury and impingement increased at debris loadings causing over 0.2 feet of head loss. The screen was rapidly cleaned of debris, however, when it was tilted to the flushing position.

As a result of Elwha's success, B.C. Hydro installed Eicher Screens during 1992 in two penstocks at the Puntledge Hydro Project in British Columbia. Preliminary results indicate that the screens at Puntledge are achieving over 99 percent diversion and survival (Smith, 1993). Total costs for construction of the Puntledge screens amounted to $4 million (U.S.) to screen 1,000 cfs, or $4,000 per cfs (about half of the cost that was estimated for installing an alternative low-velocity screening system). A cost estimate prepared in 1990 for screening the entire 2,000 cfs capacity at Elwha showed a cost of $1,500 per cfs, compared to an estimate of $3,557 per cfs for a low-velocity screening system. Data from these two sites indicate that Eicher Screens usually can be constructed at about half the cost of the low-velocity screening systems typically prescribed in the Pacific Northwest.

Modular Inclined Screen

EPRI currently is conducting a program at the Alden Research Laboratory (ARL) in Holden, Massachusetts, to develop and evaluate a modular inclined screen (MIS). The goal of the program is to develop a standardized, proven design that can be applied at nearly any type of water intake. The design has an inclined wedgewire screen mounted on a pivot shaft, contained in a rectangular module incorporating design features that provide a more uniform flow distribution than can be achieved in a penstock application. A full-sized module would contain a screen about 30 feet long by 10 feet wide inclined at an angle of 15 degrees, and would be capable of screening up to 1,000 cfs at a module velocity of 10 feet per second. Transition walls along the downstream third of the screen would taper to a 2-foot by 2-foot bypass entrance.

The MIS design was refined during hydraulic model studies conducted at ARL in a 1:6.6 scale model, and biological evaluation tests were conducted in a 1:3.3 scale model. Diversion efficiency, injury, and 3-day survival was evaluated for 10 species of fish, with the average size of test species ranging from 1.9 inches to 6.76 inches. Module velocities of 2 to 10 fps were evaluated, corresponding to an average velocity perpendicular to the screen of 0.8 to 4.0 fps.

Winchell et al. (1993) and Taft et al. (1993) summarize results of the MIS biological testing program. Detailed results were published in an EPRI report (EPRI, 1994b). Passage survival (percent diverted live and surviving for 3 days after passage) exceeded 99 percent overall for juvenile channel catfish, brown trout, coho salmon, chinook salmon and Atlantic salmon smolts.

Passage survival for most other species approached or exceeded 99 percent at velocities of up to 4 fps (bluegill and golden shiner juveniles) or 6 fps (walleye juveniles, rainbow trout fry and juveniles). The only species group with an overall passage survival of less than 95 percent was alosid juveniles (mixed blueback herring and American shad). Poor results for this species were attributed to stress caused by collection, transport, and testing.

Similar to the findings of the Eicher Screen study, test results indicated that debris accumulations causing over 0.2 feet of head loss generally resulted in an increase in injury and impingement of small fish (no impingement was observed for the relatively large Atlantic salmon smolts at a head loss of up to 0.5 feet). Again, most debris types were readily flushed by tilting the screen for a brief period, although tests conducted with pine needles found that some of them remained on the screen after flushing.

A recent comparison of six screening alternatives under consideration for a 3,000 cfs irrigation diversion in California provides cost information on construction of an MIS screening facility. Cost estimates prepared by an independent engineering firm came to $3,286 per cfs for the MIS alternative, while the five, low-velocity screening alternatives ranged between $6,947 and $12,394 per cfs.

4.2.3 Fish Bypasses at Existing Trashracks

Many downstream passage facilities prescribed in the New England area consist of bypasses installed adjacent to existing trashracks. Typically the bypasses are installed to provide an alternative to turbine passage for outmigrating Atlantic salmon smolts, juvenile American shad, and juvenile river herring (blueback herring and alewives). Because many small fish avoid passing through trashracks (Anderson, 1988, as cited in Kynard, 1993), fish migrating downstream may find and use an appropriately located bypass route.

Surface bypasses are being installed at trashracks to facilitate downstream passage at sites in the northeast, where most salmon and clupeid stocks are in a gradual rebuilding phase. Access to upstream habitat is progressively increasing as new upstream passage facilities are constructed. Because of the currently small run size of Atlantic salmon (the most highly valued stock in the northeast region) it is difficult to justify the cost of installing state-of-the-art screening facilities such as those prescribed in the Pacific Northwest. Furthermore, for the low-head projects typical on the east coast, costs of fish screening systems, which are generally proportional to the volume of flow that must be screened, are relatively high.

Appropriately located bypasses may offer an acceptable long-term method of downstream passage at sites where fish behavior under existing site conditions is conducive to achieving high bypass rates. At some sites, monitoring studies may yield information to enable simple modifications for improving bypass efficiency. At other sites, however, more extensive protective measures probably will be recommended to provide an acceptable level of protection.

Public Service of New Hampshire (PSNH) studies to develop downstream passage facilities for Atlantic salmon at five dams on the Pemigewasset and Merrimack rivers are a good example of an effective approach in the northeast. During 1989 and 1990, PSNH monitored the migration of radio-tagged salmon smolts via all potential passage routes at each dam. Results indicated that fewer than 5 percent of the smolts used bypasses installed adjacent to the project intakes (PSNH, 1992). The average proportion of fish passing via all non-turbine routes (including spillways and waste gates) ranged from 54.9 percent to 95.5 percent for the four sites where sufficient data were collected.

Follow-up studies conducted in 1991 and 1992 largely focused on improving passage at one of the dams (Ayers Island), where there was a substantial delay in outmigration during non-spill conditions. The 1992 studies found that surface spill provided by dropping a single flashboard was used by 30 of 46 smolts recorded passing the project (NUSCo, 1993). Studies to develop effective downstream passage facilities at all five dams are ongoing.

Capital costs reported for constructing fish bypass systems (see Sections 3.4.2 through 3.4.6) ranged from $9 to $12 per cfs for constructed sites (two sites), and conceptual costs of $42 to $360 per cfs were reported for four other sites (see Table 3-16). Lost generation due to providing bypass flows probably is a greater overall cost than actual construction of the bypasses. Even considering lost generation, simple bypasses are considerably less costly than state-of-the-art screening facilities. Installation of bypasses, however, does not preclude the possibility that additional measures may be recommended in the future.

4.2.4 Close-Spaced and Angled Bar Racks

Since the early 1980's, angled bar racks combined with controlled spills at a bypass facility have been one of the most commonly installed fish protection systems for hydropower projects, particularly in the northeast. Most angled bar rack facilities consist of a single bank of racks in front of the turbine intake at an angle of about 45 degrees to the flow. Although design varies from site to site, most use vertical bars oriented perpendicular to the plane of the rack with a 1-inch spacing and a bypass located at the downstream end of the rack. Generally, resource agencies specify a maximum approach velocity (perpendicular to the racks) of 2 fps and a bypass flow equivalent to 2 percent of the plant flow or 20 cfs (whichever is greater).

Most angled bar rack facilities, which have been installed at small projects (capacity less than 1,000 cfs), have not been evaluated. One performance evaluation was at the Wadhams Hydroelectric Project, a small (150 cfs capacity) project located on the Bouquet River in Wadhams, New York. The study compared passage routes of radio-tagged Atlantic salmon smolts passing the project with 1-inch spaced bar racks installed at 90 degrees and 36 degrees to the intake flow. Although sample sizes were small, the study concluded that the angled racks substantially reduced the entrainment rate of salmon smolts into the project intake (Nettles and Gloss, 1987). None of the 30 migrants passed through the penstock when the angled trashracks were in place (18 passed via the bypass and 12 passed via the spillway), while three out of six fish passed via the penstock when the racks were oriented perpendicular to the intake.

One respondent to the entrainment protection questionnaire indicated that 1-inch spaced trashracks were 100 percent effective in eliminating entrainment of landlocked Atlantic salmon at the Millinocket Pumping Station on the Penobscot River in Maine. Although trashracks did not eliminate entrainment of smelt, this was not an objective of the installation.

Although little additional data currently are available to substantiate the effectiveness of 1-inch angled bar racks, it seems likely that they would be effective in reducing the entrainment rate of larger fish capable of a sustained swimming speed of 2 fps or more simply because large fish would be physically excluded. In addition, smaller fish may avoid the turbulence created by the racks. This is the biological principal involved in the use of louvers (see Section 4.2.5), which can be effective in guiding fish that could physically pass between the louver slats. Similar to louvers, the diversion efficiency of angled bar racks probably drops off rapidly for very small fish, and some weak-swimming species may be impinged if the bar racks are not designed properly. Passage of very small fish through bar racks may not be a major concern, however, because smaller fish have low rates of turbine mortality at most sites where this was studied.

Use of trashrack overlays for reducing the entrainment rate of blueback herring was evaluated during 1992 at the Little Falls Project (RMC, 1993). Overlays, which were constructed of perforated steel plate with 0.5-inch holes, with an overall porosity of 60 percent, covered the top 20 feet (about 60 percent) of the trashracks. During testing, a range of spill flows were provided through an ice sluice located adjacent to the trashracks. Results indicated that the trashrack overlays were not effective in preventing entrainment of herring into the powerhouse. Although some increase in sluice passage was noted with increases in sluice discharge, even at the higher sluice flows more fish usually passed through the powerhouse.

Capital costs reported for construction of close-spaced bar racks with a fish bypass system (see Tables 3-14 through 3-16) was $31 to $34 per cfs for the two constructed sites, and conceptual costs ranged from $50 to $653 per cfs for another eight sites. Although angled bar rack installation has a fairly sound theoretical basis, currently there is a limited amount of quantitative data on its effectiveness.

4.2.5 Louvers

A louver system consists of an array of evenly spaced, vertical slats (normally spaced with clear openings of 1 to 12 inches) aligned across a channel at a specified angle and leading to a bypass. Because fish tend to orient themselves facing into a current, even if they are moving with it, they cannot see obstructions or barriers downstream. Fish must rely mainly on their other senses to guide them around obstacles, and louvers take advantage of this behavior. As fish approach louvers, they sense the turbulence created by the system and move laterally away from it. They are carried downstream where their lateral movement and the current eventually direct them into a bypass.

EPRI (1986) reports results of testing performed in laboratory studies and at large louver installations in Washington, Oregon, and California. Most studies showed good guidance (greater than 85 percent) for fish greater than 1.2 to 2.4 inches long, but generally much lower performance for fry. The relationship between fish length and guidance efficiency was demonstrated in the results of testing (published in 1974) at the John Skinner Fish Facility located at the intake for the California Aqueduct. The guidance efficiency at this facility decreased rapidly for striped bass less than 1.2 inches and for white catfish less than 3.6 inches

(EPRI, 1986). More recent tests conducted during the 1980's at a louver facility located at the Red Bluff Diversion dam on the Sacramento River (Vogel et al., 1990) showed a similar decrease in guidance of chinook salmon less than 2 inches long. Due to low guidance of chinook fry and predation at the existing bypass outfall, this louver facility was replaced with an angled drum screen facility in 1990.

Recently, the Northeast Utilities Service Company (NUSCo) began a major research effort to evaluate louvers for diverting juvenile and adult clupeids and Atlantic salmon smolts at the Holyoke Canal on the Connecticut River in Holyoke, Massachusetts. The canal is about 145 feet wide with a maximum flow capacity of 7,000 cfs. A 522-foot-long floating louver array was installed at an angle of about 15 degrees to the flow, with 2.5-inch wide louvers installed perpendicular to the flow at a 3-inch spacing. Effectiveness of the floating louver array was evaluated during 1990 by monitoring the migration routes of radio-tagged fish to determine whether they were guided along the length of the array to a 15-foot-wide gap at the end of the array. Louver depths of 4 to 8 feet were evaluated during the initial test program.

Testing during 1990 indicated that the floating louver array guided an average of 87 percent of Atlantic salmon smolts (NUSCo, 1990). The effectiveness of the louvers declined slightly when the louver panels were raised from their design depth of 8 feet, although the difference was not statistically significant. Tests conducted with the louver panels removed (support frame left in place) showed a guidance efficiency of 75 percent, indicating that a wider slat spacing could be effective in guiding Atlantic salmon smolts. Tests conducted with post-spawning adult

American shad also indicated successful guidance, although the results were inconclusive because shad tended to move back upstream and mill in the vicinity of the louver array (Harza and RMC, 1990).

Based on the success of the floating louver array, a permanent bypass and fish sampling facility was installed in 1992, and two modifications to the louver array were tested. In spring 1992, the louver array consisted of 402 feet of floating louvers and 40 feet of full-depth (20 feet) louvers adjacent to the bypass entrance. Studies conducted using hatchery Atlantic salmon smolts found that the guidance efficiency of the louver array was 91.3 percent with a 3-inch spacing between slats and 79.7 percent with a 12-inch spacing (Harza and RMC, 1992).

In fall 1992, an evaluation of juvenile clupeids (American shad and blueback herring) was performed at Holyoke at various canal flows with a non-floating louver facility. The facility consisted of 400 feet of 9-foot-deep, 2-inch spaced louvers plus 40 feet of full depth (20 feet) louvers adjacent to the bypass. The study found that 76 percent of marked and recaptured test fish were guided, and 86 percent of naturally migrating fish were guided into the bypass (Harza and RMC, 1993).

The non-floating facility described above was evaluated with hatchery and wild Atlantic salmon smolts at various canal flows. The report is currently in preparation, but data indicate that the overall effectiveness was between 85 percent and 90 percent.

Total project cost for construction and evaluation of the various louver configurations tested at Holyoke was approximately $6 million, about half of which was incurred during evaluation studies. With a canal capacity of 7,000 cfs, this is a cost of about $857 per cfs for the total program and $428 per cfs for installation of the louvers alone.

4.2.6 Barrier Nets

Barrier nets are potentially a lower cost method of reducing fish entrainment rates. About half of the installations, however, have been ineffective and/or have needed extensive maintenance efforts due to biofouling, debris loading, excessive velocities, and/or wave action. Barrier nets prevent or reduce entrainment of resident species, but do not usually incorporate any type of bypass for movement downstream from the dam.

In 1983 and 1984, evaluation of a barrier net installed at the J. R. Whiting plant in Michigan indicated that the net reduced impingement of gizzard shad and yellow perch on the 3/8-inch traveling screens (located behind the barrier net) by 89 to 95 percent and 94 to 97 percent, respectively, from levels reported in 1978 and 1979 before barrier net installation (CPC, 1985). Monitoring studies conducted in 1984 indicated that overall impingement rates (a measure of how many fish passed through or around the net at this steam electric plant) decreased by 97 to 99 percent compared to the same years.

An extensive 2-year evaluation was also performed of a barrier net installed during the ice-free season at the Pine Hydroelectric Project in Wisconsin. Full-flow netting of the power canal indicated that the total entrainment rate was reduced by about 70 percent (SWEC, 1991; EPRI, 1992b). Many fish were captured in the first month after the net was deployed, suggesting that most of these fish resided

downstream of the net at the time it was deployed. Larger fish (greater than 4 inches long) were excluded based on results of mark-recapture studies, which indicated a 92 percent reduction in the entrainment rate for this size range. Effectiveness of the barrier net might have been greater if the net extended to the water surface, but due to debris loading concerns, the net was deployed 12 to 18 inches below the surface. The net is scheduled to be redeployed in 1994 or 1995.

A large barrier net (2.5 miles long) has been used at the Ludington Pumped Storage plant on Lake Michigan since 1989. Evaluation studies conducted during 1989 to 1990 indicated 30 to 37 percent overall effectiveness; however, the effectiveness improved to 77 to 84 percent in 1991 to 1992 (CPC and Detroit Edison Company, 1992).

Other installations where barrier nets have been less effective include the Quad Cities Station on the Mississippi River and the Eastlake Generating Station on Lake Erie. Debris loading and biofouling caused extensive problems at the Quad Cities barrier net (LMS, 1986). Wave action, debris loading, and shifting substrate caused similar problems at the Eastlake Generating Station (Environmental Resource Associates, Inc., 1984, cited in LMS, 1986).

Cost information on barrier nets is only available for Pine, where design, construction, and installation of the net cost approximately $35,000, or $56 per cfs of plant capacity. Operation and maintenance costs are approximately $2,000 to 3,000 per year (including periodic net replacement); these costs could be substantially higher at sites with greater debris loading.

4.2.7 Behavioral Barriers

There has been extensive research on the use of behavioral devices including sound, lights, and electrical fields for protecting fish at water intakes. EPRI (1986) summarizes much of the earlier work, and detailed information on more recent studies is presented in an update to the 1986 report (EPRI, 1994a).

Results obtained with most behavioral devices have been highly variable. All known behavioral guidance systems are experimental installations, although some systems currently being evaluated probably will be incorporated into permanent installations. The most promising results, although highly species-specific, have been obtained with strobe lights and transducer sound systems. In the following section we summarize several test programs that have demonstrated effective fish guidance with behavioral devices.

Strobe lights show good promise for diverting outmigrating juvenile American shad and possibly Atlantic salmon smolts. Tests conducted at the York Haven Hydroelectric Project on the Susquehanna River in Pennsylvania showed that strobe lights are highly effective for repelling shad into an ice sluiceway used as a fish bypass. Outmigrating shad at this site tend to avoid passing through the trashracks at the turbine intakes, and large numbers of fish accumulate at the end of the intake canal during low-spill years. Test results from 1991 indicated that an average of 1,712 shad passed through the sluiceway during each 2-minute strobe test, while the average sluiceway passage during control periods with the same sluiceway flow was only 38 fish (EPRI, 1992c). Metropolitan Edison is continuing studies to develop a permanent bypass system using strobe lights at this site.

Studies conducted at Weldon dam on the Penobscot River indicate that strobe lights may divert Atlantic salmon smolts. In 1988, strobe lights were installed at the intake to one unit, and the passage rate of smolts through a fish bypass pipe at the unit were evaluated with and without the strobe lights in operation. The results showed that 78 percent fewer smolts entered the bypass pipe when the strobe lights were operating (GPC, 1988). As a result, strobe lights have been incorporated into a new fish bypass system installed during 1992. The bypass system incorporates 1-inch spaced bar racks at all four units, bypass facilities at the two near-shore units, and strobe lights to repel fish from the intakes of the other two units. Evaluation studies are ongoing.

Two patented sound projection systems have recently been evaluated. Developers of both systems customize the sound level and frequency to optimize the response of the target species. The sound system developed by the American Electric Power Corp. yielded the best results at the Buchanan Hydroelectric Project on the St. Joseph River in Michigan. The sound system was deployed in the project's headrace, and its effectiveness was monitored by comparing the catch rates in nets deployed immediately downstream of the sound projectors (total passage rates into the headrace were not evaluated). Although few fish were caught in the nets, test results indicated that 94 percent fewer steelhead smolts and 81 percent fewer chinook smolts were caught in the nets when the sound system was operating (Loeffelman et al., 1991; Klinect et al., 1992).

Sonalysts Incorporated developed a second, patented sound system. Testing conducted at the James A. Fitzpatrick Nuclear Plant on Lake Ontario showed that at maximum circulating pump operation, a full-scale sound system resulted in an 87 percent decrease in alewife impingement (Ross et al., in press). The Sonalysts system also showed potential for diverting juvenile American shad. Testing conducted during 1992 at the Vernon Hydroelectric Project on the Connecticut River demonstrated that outmigrating shad showed a strong avoidance response to the sound system (RMC, 1993).

Because there are few data on operation of full-scale behavioral guidance systems, there is little cost information available. Based on the cost of the components involved, however, full-scale strobe light or sound systems probably could be deployed for between $100,000 and $1,000,000 for a 10,000 cfs capacity plant, or about $10 to $100 per cfs. Results to date indicate, however, that behavioral systems may not be effective for some target species, and that evaluation studies may be required to demonstrate effectiveness.

4.3 Entrainment Rates Relative to Impoundment Populations

Abundance of many species in impoundments relative to entrained species (see Section 3.3) probably can be attributed to habitat preferences and behavioral patterns. The position of the plant intake plays a major role in which species are most often entrained. For example, a relatively shallow impoundment with much aquatic vegetation is ideally suited to centrarchids. If the project intake is located in relatively deep water and away from spawning and nursery areas, however, entrainment rates of centrarchids would probably be low.

Conversely, an impoundment as a whole may be relatively poor centrarchid habitat, but if the project intake is located near good spawning and nursery habitat, the number of entrained centrarchids could be relatively high, especially when the juveniles leave the nests in mid- to late summer or when the aquatic vegetation associated with nursery areas dies back in the fall (most entrained centrarchids are juveniles). Habitat mapping conducted at some of the Au Sable and Muskegon river projects (especially Five Channels) and the King Mill Project supports this explanation.

There is not enough information available to support broad generalizations about the relationship of impoundment populations to entrainment rates. Most population estimates are conducted on adult resident sportfish, and most entrained fish are juveniles. If the population of a species in an impoundment is relatively high, however, such as the 19 walleye per acre (3- to 26- inches long) at Crowley, the number of entrained juveniles of that species also is probably relatively high (Table 3-10).

High densities of adults create situations where density-dependent mechanisms limit the number of juvenile fish that reach adulthood. Mechanisms include increased predation and migration from the impoundment. The degree of outmigration probably is influenced by how close the impoundment is to its carrying capacity and behavioral characteristics of the species. For example, juvenile walleye tend to be more pelagic than juvenile sunfish. Therefore, young walleye outmigration probably is more important than predation as a density controlling factor for this species. An intake in open water (removed from shoreline habitat) would probably show high walleye entrainment rates when the density of adults is high in the impoundment.

Young sunfish are most frequently found in shallow water habitats with at least some cover, and when sufficient cover is present, they are generally not found in open water. Consequently, entrainment rates of sunfish at a plant with an intake in open water probably would not be high, even when the density of adults is near the carrying capacity of the impoundment. There is insufficient information in the reports about habitat near the intakes of the five sites in the database for which there are population data, however, to test this hypothesis.

4.4 Suggested Guidelines for Determining the Need for Entrainment Studies

The need for entrainment studies must be established during the early stages of consultations between the licensee/applicant and the state and federal resource agencies. First, the potentially affected resource must be characterized.

Entrainment studies may not be necessary if the impoundment management objectives are being met or exceeded. To assess this, an up-to-date fisheries management plan with specific, quantifiable management objectives must be in place. Later, management plans may be revised if state outdoor recreational studies indicate that there is a deficiency in fishing opportunities. Revisions to fisheries management objectives are normally independent of hydroplant operations, however, and are supported by demographic data.

Entrainment studies also may not be necessary where fisheries resources are not exploitable. For example, fishing has been banned in the Upper Hudson River where there are unacceptably high levels of toxicants. In such a case, a restoration plan is established that schedules clean-up and follow-up testing to ensure that toxicant levels in the environment have returned to acceptable levels. Elements in the restoration schedule may be used to trigger consideration of the need for entrainment studies.

Inaccessibility may eliminate the immediate need for an entrainment study. If downstream-accessible fisheries depend on upstream recruitment of fish that must pass by a project, however, the need for entrainment studies is greater.

Entrainment studies also may be unnecessary if, as it is in some cases, some cropping of "rough fish" during entrainment may improve conditions for other species. Sometimes this phenomena combined with minor adverse impacts of entrainment on existing or proposed fisheries would not justify either the cost of studies or installing protective measures.

Occasionally, the potentially affected fisheries resource has such a high value that protective measures do not need to be justified (e.g., on rivers that support anadromous populations of Atlantic or Pacific salmonids). At these sites, however, studies are increasingly recommended to evaluate the effectiveness after the protective measures are implemented. The potential mortality associated with bypass options relative to turbine mortality may be a consideration.

If need cannot be ruled out, a study may be appropriate to determine whether or not the magnitude of the entrainment at a specific site warrants protective measures. Alternatively, protective measures could be installed without conducting entrainment studies.

A need assessment first establishes what types of protective measures might be most effective at a specific site given the resources. Resource agencies and other parties provide input to estimate the nature of the potentially affected resource. Such input may include: 1) results of studies on the composition of the fish community of the impoundment, 2) fisheries management plans, 3) recent creel census data, 4) stocking records, 5) water quality and sediment testing results, and 6) rare species records.

The licensee/applicant and/or resource agencies may suggest protective measures that seem feasible for the physical configuration of the power plant and its electrical generation objectives. One or two reasonable protective measures may be agreed upon for further exploration based on studies at similarly configured projects.

Francfort et al. (1994) indicate that for a typical 10 MW project generating 41 million kWh/year, installation costs of a screen/bypass system would average about $600,000, and total annual costs would average about $82,000 for the first 20 years of operation. Installation of angled racks at an identical project would average $220,000, and total annual costs would average $25,000. Francfort et al. (1994) also provide costs for downstream protective measures versus plant generating capacity, which can serve as a basis for preliminary decisions on whether to further explore protective measures or consider conducting entrainment studies.

Estimated conceptual costs for the most reasonable protective measures then should be developed. The design costs associated with developing such estimates typically range from $1,500 to $20,000, unless the proposed protective measure involves research and development (see Tables 3-12 and 3-13). Conceptual costs probably will include:

- the capital costs associated with installing the protective measure;

- an accurate estimate of operation and maintenance costs during the term of the new license;

- the costs of lost generation during construction and operation; and

- the expected cost of evaluating the effectiveness of the protective measure, if recommended, based on current agency policy in the region.

The conceptual costs associated with implementing a protective measure can be compared to the potentially achievable resource benefit. If the potential resource benefit justifies the protective measure, the licensee/applicant may forgo entrainment studies and install the measure. If the potential resource benefit is uncertain, but has a good likelihood of justifying the protective measure, then installation costs can be compared to the estimated costs of conducting entrainment studies. Most entrainment studies that have gained agency approval involve either netting or netting combined with hydroacoustics. The costs associated with such studies vary but often range between $300,000 and $500,000 (see Table 3-11). These are probably minimum costs, given recently issued guidelines for conducting entrainment studies in Michigan, Wisconsin, and Pennsylvania and the potential that additional assessments would be recommended if parts of the original study are not conclusive or do not meet with agency approval.

Estimated costs for entrainment studies can be reduced considerably if extrapolation of study results to other sites is appropriate.

4.5 Suggested Guidelines for Conducting Entrainment Studies

When the need to conduct site-specific entrainment studies is clearly identified, methods to achieve study objectives should be established. A standardized approach to methods and reporting entrainment data at specific sites may allow meaningful comparisons with other studies. Progress towards such standardization has been made in Michigan and Wisconsin with the issuance of the "Joint Agency Fish Entrainment/Turbine Mortality Study Plan Guidelines" by the USFWS and the Wisconsin and Michigan Departments of Natural Resources (1992).

Some standardization recommendations may be applied outside of a region, but detailed standards are best developed regionally to account for local resource values. We recommend flexible guidelines that can be modified based on consultations between the licensee/applicant and the resource agencies. Sampling conditions are often unique, however, and may require deviations from a standardized sampling protocol so that study objectives can be achieved. Licensees/applicants and the agencies should agree on as many study details as possible before the study begins to ensure that the collected data address project objectives. FERC is available to resolve disputes if study plans or need for studies cannot be agreed upon.

Before a study begins, the minimum size of fish to include in the entrainment estimate must be defined. USFWS et al. (1992) suggested limiting entrainment estimates in Michigan and Wisconsin to all fish greater than 1.5 inches (38 mm) long. Adoption of this criteria would have substantially reduced the annual entrainment estimates at the three Wisconsin River sites in the database. It would have increased annual entrainment estimates at those sites where the minimum detectable fish, based on hydroacoustic techniques, were considerably greater than 1.5 inches.

If hydroacoustic estimates are adjusted using representative net collections (as was done in several studies at South Carolina sites conducted by Duke Power), then annual entrainment rate is less likely to be underestimated. Regardless of minimum fish size, the estimates are most useful when results can be compared regionally and/or basin-wide.

The most appropriate method for collecting entrainment samples at a specific site, usually netting and/or hydroacoustic techniques, must be identified. Each method has advantages and disadvantages, and, frequently, combining both techniques can minimize disadvantages. Major advantages of netting are that data on species, size classes, and (when tailrace netting is used) condition of entrained fish can be obtained. Disadvantages include high cost (which frequently limits the temporal coverage of sampling), potential damage to otherwise healthy fish from collection and handling, and uncertainty of results (intrusion of non-entrained fish and escapement of entrained fish from the net).

Advantages of hydroacoustic methods are that information on entrainment can be collected over a much broader temporal and spatial spectrum than is practical for netting, there is no collection mortality of fish, and the cost of studies is generally less than for netting. Disadvantages include uncertainty as to the species of fish detected, inability to effectively sample in high noise situations, occasional false fish counts, and use of a complex technology that requires specialized training. Also, agencies that review results sometimes are unwilling to accept hydroacoustic entrainment results (see Appendix 3.2).

Much recent resource agency reluctance to accept hydroacoustic entrainment estimates is based on *"Acoustic Estimation of Fish Entrainment, Analysis of Sources of Error - With Special Reference to Wisconsin Entrainment Projects"* (Thorne, 1992). This report, prepared for the Wisconsin Department of Natural Resources, highlights potential sources of error in unattended hydroacoustic studies conducted in the midwest during the mid- to late 1980's. Many problems originated from applying hydroacoustic approaches that were successful on large, western rivers (such as the Columbia River) to small hydropower plants typically found in Wisconsin. Entrainment at Wisconsin hydropower projects is more complex than at most western sites because there is often more noise; surface-oriented intakes and resultant potential for false counts from air bubbles and ice break-up; increased fish species of concern; variable size and behavior of entrained fish; the need to conduct studies for much of the year rather than just during salmonid outmigration periods; and operational differences that can create false counts, such as trashrack cleaning with rakes or air jets. Thorne (1992) emphasizes that, when comparing acoustics and netting, costs, achievable precision, and fish mortalities must be considered. He indicates that, in most

cases, inaccuracies in hydroacoustics can be overcome by proper experimental design. This may increase cost of hydroacoustic studies at midwest sites (and other locations with similar characteristics). Thorne contends, however, that properly designed hydroacoustic studies can produce more accurate entrainment estimates than netting studies of similar (or greater) cost.

Studies in the database indicate that it may be inappropriate to assume that the entrainment rate at a sampled unit is similar to that at unsampled units, especially if one unit is located along a shoreline and the others are located mid-river, or if the intake structure is parallel to the prevailing flow. Entrainment rate at one unit is more likely to be similar to another unit if both are located at mid-river; this cannot, however, be confirmed with available information. If there is more than one operating turbine, sampling at least two turbines may be appropriate unless a basis can be agreed upon for sampling only one unit. Sampling at one unit should produce a conservative estimate of the entrainment rate (higher or equal to actual entrainment rates) when extrapolated to the other units.

Where several intake structures extend from near the shoreline, sampling the shoreline intake alone may yield a conservative entrainment estimate. Two studies in the database (Shawano and Greenup Lock and Dam) support this approach. Several other studies suggest that more fish are entrained adjacent to structures (i.e., walls) than in open areas, which also may support sampling at shoreline-oriented intakes because the shoreline would also represent a structure. Also, many species of fish (e.g., centrarchids, pickerel, and minnows) are more often found in near-shore habitats. If an impoundment is dominated by such species, sampling only a shoreline intake may provide the most conservative estimate.

If an intake is parallel to the prevailing flow, netting may be appropriate at more than one turbine to account for species-specific behavioral patterns that would not be detected by hydroacoustics. For example, minnows seemed to be entrained at the upstream portion of the intake at Station 26, whereas gizzard shad were entrained at the downstream end.

The number of units to be sampled is best agreed upon during agency consultation. When only net collections are used, assumptions necessary to extrapolate to unsampled units can be identified before beginning the study.

Using hydroacoustics along with netting may be a cost-effective method for accurately estimating entrainment rates at plants with multiple units. For example, the Beaver Falls study indicates that unit-specific entrainment rates may be substantially influenced by whether or not the adjacent unit is operating. When the adjacent unit was operating, the overall entrainment rate declined substantially. Extrapolating from one unit to the other in this case, according to the consultant conducting this study, would have been unrealistically conservative. The operational status of each turbine during sampling must be accurately documented, even if each unit is not sampled.

Feasibility of the proposed sampling technique at each site can be verified by what USFWS et al. (1992) call a "proof-of-concept" (POC) study. Sometimes after a study is completed, the licensee/applicant and/or the agencies note that the results of one or more aspects of the study were not usable. If a brief POC study had been implemented to verify effectiveness first, considerable time and expense could have been saved. POC studies are best conducted when a sufficient quantity of entrainable fish are expected at the site. Monthly entrainment data in the database provide guidance as to when entrainment rates may be highest in different parts of the country. Alternatively, hatchery fish can be used as long as their size and behavioral characteristics are representative of fish likely to be entrained. The results of POC studies can be reviewed by appropriate state and federal agencies and the methodology approved before beginning the entrainment study.

4.5.1 Guidelines for Netting Studies

A major advantage of sampling with nets is that the species and size distribution of entrained fish can be characterized. Voucher specimens of each species captured, except for rare or endangered species, can be preserved to verify identifications.

Full-Flow Tailrace Net Installations

The most reliable entrainment data are obtained when the entire flow exiting from at least one turbine is sampled. The net is usually attached to a rigid frame that is securely positioned against the tailrace bay of the powerhouse (dewatering slots, if present, are often an ideal anchoring location for the frame). Attaching the netting directly to the powerhouse at a few points, as was done at Constantine, may cause the net to billow and potentially increase escapement and intrusion of fish, thereby lowering net collection efficiency.

Before finalizing the tailrace position to be sampled, the tailrace can be surveyed by divers during the POC study to identify underwater obstructions that could damage the nets and invalidate sampling. Most collection nets have at least a 1:3 width-to-length ratio, which enables definition of the area to be surveyed by the diver. If obstructions cannot be moved, the sampling location may need to be altered. If not possible, heavy canvas can be installed on the outside of the net to reduce damage, but the nets must then be checked for damage frequently. Once the net is in place, it can be checked by a diver for any gaps between the netting and the powerhouse. Gaps then can be sealed before sampling begins using sandbags, metal panels, PVC pipes, foam seal, or rubber boots (EPRI, 1992b).

Partial-flow Net Installations

Sometimes it is not possible to install full-flow tailrace nets, e.g., at plants with high discharges or tailraces that are inaccessible for safe sampling. Partial-flow netting may be the only alternative. Partial-flow netting ideally should be placed in front of the turbines where the water velocity is such that fish are committed to entrainment (usually 3 to 6 fps, depending on the species of concern). Flow meters installed in forebay nets can document the velocity and compare it to typical swimming speeds (burst speeds) of collected fish. Unfortunately, the preferred high-velocity sampling zone often is behind the trashracks, which can cause serious damage to the turbines if nets break loose; use of sturdy nets will reduce this potential. At some plants, a stationary screen behind the nets can be installed during sampling to minimize the risk of turbine damage. Because samples collected in front of the trashracks may sample fish not committed to entrainment, water velocity data at the collection point is especially important. Such data can be used to assess the degree

to which non-entrained fish may influence entrainment rate estimates.

Partial-flow netting is least effective in the tailrace because it is not possible to distinguish tailrace intruders from entrained fish, which can seriously affect the accuracy of the data.

Net Design

Although the studies in the database provide general characteristics for the design of entrainment nets, site-specific conditions often dictate final net design. Many full-flow netting studies in the database used a larger meshed chaffing net (0.75- to 1.50-inch bar mesh) to cover and protect a finer meshed collection net from the considerable turbulence full-flow tailrace nets are subject to. This finer meshed net sometimes lines the entire net, and sometimes only the rear half or third of the net.

Mesh sizes cited in the database ranged from 0.25-inch bar mesh (at nine sites) to 1.5-inch bar mesh (at Escanaba dams 1 and 3). USFWS et al. (1992) guidelines for Michigan and Wisconsin specify 0.25-inch bar mesh knotless nylon nets. Using a small meshed net limits intrusion or extrusion of fish through the mesh. The extra drag created by the small mesh could increase net billowing, however, especially at high discharges, and may force entrained fish through any small gaps between the net and the powerhouse.

Maintaining a small meshed net in a high discharge tailrace may be difficult if not impossible because of excessive drag. Eight of the nine sites that used 0.25-inch mesh indicate that the flow through each net ranged from 180 cfs (Tower) to approximately 600 cfs (Crowley) and averaged 360 cfs; through-net flow could not be estimated at King Mill. Collection efficiency at these sites was high, and at Tower, Kleber, Crowley, and Shawano it exceeded 80 percent. At Buchanan, Constantine, and French Landing (a partial-flow tailrace netting site), collection efficiency was generally under 60 percent, which could reflect drag-related problems.

The results at Crowley indicate that it is possible to successfully use 0.25-inch knotless nylon mesh nets under conditions that sample up to 600 cfs if the net is sturdy. The net showed obvious signs of stress, and an extension was added to reduce the stress on the mesh and frame attachment points. Increasing the length of the net effectively allows 0.25-inch mesh to be used under relatively high flow conditions. When through-net flows exceed 500 cfs, an evaluation of netting with a full 0.25-inch mesh liner may be needed in the POC study. A removable liner in the front portion of the net allows a relatively inexpensive evaluation of both netting options.

The most appropriate mesh size is a function of site-specific conditions and study objectives. Sampling difficulty is more likely to be a factor, however, when 0.25-inch mesh is used. If large fish entrainment is the primary study objective, using a larger mesh size for netting studies could produce more representative results. Interpreting the importance of collecting large quantities of small fish is difficult because entrainment survival of small fish is typically high. The population impacts of limited entrainment mortality on small fish are questionable.

Tailrace nets can be equipped with live cars to allow fish to be returned to the river unharmed after processing, provide fish to be used in collection efficiency studies, and enable assessment of turbine mortality. EPRI (1992b) describes typical live-car construction. Sewing a fyke into the rear portion of the net will minimize potential for collected fish to escape. Also, many collection nets used in database studies were dark colored which reduced the potential for fish avoidance.

Tailrace Net Presample Flushing

Before tailrace net sampling begins, the unit to be sampled is normally shut down to install the nets. When the unit is restarted, the nets are usually set for a brief period to allow non-entrained fish to be flushed from the net before sampling. The amount of time used to flush the nets varied from 15 minutes at studies conducted by Duke Power to several hours at Crowley. The time needed to flush tailrace residents from the tailrace bay depends on the plant configuration; plants with areas of dead water or eddies would be expected to take longer to flush than more streamlined arrangements. Fish collected during flushing should be counted and recorded to indicate the adequacy of the flushing period. Low numbers of fish in the flush sample suggest that the duration of the flush sample is appropriate. If a flush sample has an uncharacteristically high number of fish relative to previous flush samples, the flushing period may need to be lengthened.

Exclusion of Fish From Entrainment Estimates

Most netting studies exclude certain fish from the entrainment estimates based on criteria that identify the fish as not having been entrained. Exclusion criteria include fish that are too wide to fit through the trashracks (determined by direct measurement or by developing species-specific length-width relationships based on representative samples) and fish that are known to occur only in the tailwaters.

Accepting these exclusions acknowledges tailrace intrusion of fish, however, which raises questions about the adequacy of the seal of the net against the powerhouse.

The licensee/applicant and agencies should agree which fish can be appropriately excluded from the entrainment estimate during study design consultations. Performance standards can be developed early in the sampling program to specify corrective actions if the number of tailrace intruders becomes excessive. Some entrainment studies also excluded fish that were "obviously dead prior to entrainment." This may be appropriate for fish that are decomposing at the time of collection, but can be subjective for fish that have not been dead for long. The criteria characterizing fish that are dead before entrainment can be established before study implementation or as soon as a problem is noted.

At some sites (e.g., Youghiogheny and Buzzard's Roost), entrainment rates increased substantially during the winter. The licensee/applicant hypothesized that many of these fish were thermally stressed and either dead or dying when entrained and that inclusion of these fish in assessing impact of the hydroelectric plant was inappropriate without substantive evidence; agencies may not support this approach. Continuously monitoring forebay water temperature during the winter and forebay netting at a location where the velocity is low enough to enable healthy fish to escape may help support the licensee/applicant's case.

Net Efficiency Studies

Net efficiency studies help determine what proportion of fish passing through a turbine are collected by the sampling net. Results of these studies are used to adjust entrainment rate estimates to account for

fish that escape collection and to trigger repairs to the net or other corrective measures.

Efficiency tests are most useful if conducted regularly and should use both live and dead fish that represent the sizes and species of fish likely to be entrained. Test fish should be marked and measured to distinguish them from non-test fish. Test fish may be either of wild or hatchery origin, and resource agencies should be consulted to select representative species and sizes. Incorporating at least one net efficiency study into the POC study is appropriate.

Test fish are released either directly in front of the turbines, the mouth of the collection net, or both; the most appropriate location depends on site-specific conditions. Most database studies (12 of 21) released fish in front of the turbines. Through-turbine releases most closely simulate how naturally entrained fish will be collected and can readily be combined with turbine mortality studies. Results may be inaccurate if fish are released where the velocity is insufficient to ensure that all fish are entrained (a parameter not readily quantified when live fish are released), fish passage is delayed due to back-eddies or areas of dead water within the plant (as at Tower and Kleber), or if sampled and unsampled tailrace bays are interconnected.

Releases directly into the mouth of the net provide greater assurance that fish will be collected and that they cannot escape before passage through the turbines or via unsampled turbine bays. Fish released into the mouth of the net may not behave the same as entrained fish, however, and the spatial distribution of fish released at a single point may be different from entrained fish, especially if the point of release is not appropriate. Through-turbine releases are preferable to net-mouth releases if a review of the plant configuration (diagrams and site visits) indicates that the above-mentioned disadvantages can be minimized. For example, fish released into a net can be released at the point of maximum velocity (as determined by flow meter).

Test fish can be introduced via a suitably designed system that ensures all fish are released at the designated location. Typical release systems include a test fish holding tank, tubing from the tank to the release point, and a flushing mechanism or plunger. Test releases of at least 50 fish per species, and uniform condition (live or dead) and size class increase the accuracy of results. Control fish are also needed to accurately assess turbine mortality if this is a study objective. Separate tests can be considered for each collection net. If the turbine(s) to be sampled typically operate at different hydraulic rates, then tests that represent the expected range of flows may be appropriate. For full-flow netting, an effective collection efficiency exceeds 85 percent; if it is less than 70 percent, corrective action must be considered.

We recommend at least two separate net efficiency studies (including the POC study) conducted at roughly evenly spaced time intervals. We recommend evaluation of net efficiency more frequently (perhaps on a reduced scale, using fish collected during routine sampling) because corrective action needs can be quickly assessed (e.g., when a net is torn or the seal between the net and the powerhouse is disrupted) and the chance that sampling will be invalid is reduced. Net efficiency studies were conducted once a month at the five Duke Power sites in the database. This frequency enabled identification of any net problems that developed during the study.

The availability of appropriate fish, on-site sampling conditions (e.g., ice or flood flows make sampling hazardous, excessive stress to fish), and cost must be considered when designing net efficiency studies. Such factors influence the number of fish per efficiency test release and the frequency of testing.

Collection efficiency data normally is used to adjust entrainment rates. Because collection efficiency may change over time (reflecting changes in plant operating mode, condition of the net, and/or shifts in the size or species of entrained fish), the sampling period and operating conditions represented by each efficiency test is typically specified. Collection efficiency for each test species and size class is also clearly presented. Test species used as surrogates should have similar body shapes and swimming ability to the species they represent.

Sampling Schedule

Specific objectives of entrainment studies determine the frequency and duration of sampling. An estimate of the annual number and sizes of each species of fish entrained generally indicates whether protective measures are appropriate at a specific site. If modifying plant operations (e.g., restricting plant operations during periods of high entrainment rates) is a possible protective measure, however, then entrainment rate estimates for more specific time periods should be developed (e.g., monthly and/or hourly). Monthly sampling efforts of studies in the database ranged from 1 to 30 days. Generally, 1 day of sampling per month characterized periods when low entrainment rates were expected (usually winter). At some sites (especially those dominated by clupeids), however, entrainment rates were often the highest during the winter, which illustrates the importance of acquiring information on the fish community before designing site-specific entrainment studies. Sampling efforts during spring, summer, and fall (periods when fish activity is expected to be high) was typically 3 to 6 days per month at most sites.

Derr et al. (1993) discuss in detail factors to consider in establishing entrainment sampling schedules. Their recommendations were based on a review of data from the most comprehensive study in the database, Youghiogheny. Both units at this site were sampled continuously with full-flow tailrace nets for 1 year. They emphasize the importance of establishing decision criteria (such as desired levels of precision and acceptable levels of bias) for proposed studies by close coordination between agency personnel and those conducting the studies. Bias can be introduced by annual, seasonal, diurnal, site-specific (i.e., differences between units), and net sampling efficiency factors. The first three factors are discussed below, the other two factors are addressed earlier in this section.

Annual factors can create bias relative to whether or not the year selected for study is representative of other years. To estimate variation from year to year the site must be monitored for more than 1 year (Derr et al., 1993). Section 3.2.1 indicates the nature of variation in entrainment rates between years. At sites with more than 1 year of data, the relative abundance of species was generally similar from year to year as was the timing and, in some cases, the magnitude of seasonal peak entrainment rates. Monitoring entrainment for more than 1 year is the best way to minimize biases due to annual factors, but frequently, this may not be practical due to high cost. Physical factors, such as river discharge, flow through the plant, and/or water

temperature, also may be monitored to determine whether the year sampled is typical of non-sampled years. If considered typical (as defined by consultation), results from one year may be considered representative of other years.

Seasonal bias factors can be considered if sampling efforts vary for each month. Derr et al. (1993) emphasize the importance of using available regional data and expert opinions to help minimize this type of bias. They also indicate that using a flexible sampling program enables the sampling regime to be adjusted based on the results of POC studies (referred to by Derr as pilot studies). For example, if sampling is proposed for 1 or 2 days a month during winter and the first sampling effort shows a collection of large numbers of fish, it would be appropriate to increase the level of sampling.

Maximizing precision while minimizing the amount of sampling depends on the "autocorrelation" relationship of entrainment (Derr et al., 1993). Autocorrelation, which is the dependence of one day's counts to the counts on a subsequent day, also affects the precision of the estimate of monthly mean entrainment rates. Derr et al.'s analysis of the Youghiogheny data for December and January suggested that there was strong autocorrelation during these 2 months. Given this dependence, sampling at regular rather than consecutive intervals would increase the precision of the entrainment rate estimate with the least amount of sampling effort and provide narrower confidence intervals. At Youghiogheny, sampling every fifth or sixth day (5 or 6 days per month) would have produced an adequately precise (conforming to pre-established criteria) estimate of the mean entrainment rate. This sampling frequency also would probably have detected peak entrainment events at Youghiogheny.

USFWS et al. (1992) guidelines for Michigan and Wisconsin specify conducting net sampling for 3 days a week at each unit sampled from April to October, and 3 days every 2 weeks for the rest of the year. The impact to entrained fish of sampling at such frequent intervals may be considerable, given the stress and mortality often associated with net sampling, and the costs associated with such a rigorous sampling regime should be considered.

If netting is used to verify hydroacoustic sampling, USFWS et al. (1992) recommend 1 day per week from April to October and 1 day every other week for the rest of the year. Derr et al. (1993) stress the importance of having a statistician work with biologists to design the appropriate sampling frequency.

Based on the prevalence of sites in the database with episodic entrainment, we recommend spacing sampling days at regular intervals rather than consecutively. The number of days sampled per month can balance good experimental design with the sample collection cost. We also recommend that a sample consist of no more than 24 hours of data collection, which will standardize collection efforts. Sampling for several days without checking the nets can cause nets to become clogged with debris and increase mortality of fish collected due to sampling-related stress. Results of such collections may not be comparable to results from samples collected for up to 24 hours.

Millville was the only other site (besides Youghiogheny) where a sufficient number of days were sampled with a full-flow net to evaluate the effect of sampling frequency on the accuracy of entrainment

rate estimates. We performed a cursory analysis using the 1991 Millville data (Table 4-1) to assess the error associated with sampling 3 randomly selected days per month versus 3 consecutive days. We selected 5 months in which over 10 days of sampling was performed for this analysis (range: 11 to 25 days). Ten trials were performed in which 3 days were randomly selected from each month's data (data were not available to allow selection of uniformly spaced sampling dates), and we performed another 10 trials in which we randomly selected a string of 3 consecutive days (or as close to consecutive as the data allowed).

We compared the average entrainment rate over the 15 days selected in each trial to the average of the monthly entrainment rates using all available data. The degree of error (deviation from the mean using all data) averaged 8.65 percent (range: 1.4 percent to 17.7 percent) when we randomly selected the three individual sampling dates per month. The average error increased to 35.3 percent (range: 9.3 percent to 100.5 percent) when we selected strings of 3 consecutive days. The error for estimates of the entrainment rate for individual months or species of fish is likely to be greater. This analysis supports Derr et al.'s conclusion that the error can be reduced substantially by avoiding sampling on consecutive days. It also indicates the level of error associated with sampling 3 consecutive days per month, which has been used in many of the studies conducted to date. Sampling on nonconsecutive days generally increases the cost of an entrainment study, but costs may be offset by sampling fewer days while maintaining or decreasing estimate error.

TABLE 4-1
1991 MILLVILLE ENTRAINMENT DATA USED TO EVALUATE THE ERROR ASSOCIATED WITH SAMPLING THREE DAYS PER MONTH (CONSECUTIVE OR INDEPENDENT) SOURCE: EEM (1992)

Collections			Collections			Collections		
Date	Fish	Hours	Date	Fish	Hours	Date	Fish	Hours
1/24/91	5	23.8	6/10/91	476	24.3	10/14/91	22	22.7
1/25/91	15	19.0	6/12/91	88	21.8	10/15/91	44	22.5
1/29/91	2	25.8	6/15/91	167	21.6	10/16/91	36	23.1
1/30/91	1	25.0	6/18/91	64	23.8	10/17/91	17	24.8
1/31/91	1	24.0	6/19/91	76	23.8	10/18/91	25	23.6
2/02/91	1	18.6	6/20/91	77	24.1	10/19/91	26	22.9
2/03/91	0	19.6	6/21/91	89	23.8	10/20/91	29	24.2
2/04/91	0	20.6	6/22/91	71	20.0	10/21/91	43	24.3
2/05/91	1	24.0	6/23/91	166	24.3	10/22/91	16	23.7
2/07/91	0	23.6	6/24/91	110	25.1	10/23/91	17	21.1
2/08/91	0	24.6	6/25/91	37	23.8	10/24/91	2	22.4
2/09/91	2	24.5	6/26/91	103	23.9	10/31/91	44	27.7
2/10/91	0	23.8	6/28/91	2	22.1	11/01/91	34	15.7
2/11/91	3	24.2	7/03/91	45	21.5	11/02/91	59	24.7
2/14/91	1	21.0	7/04/91	39	24.2	11/03/91	34	23.8
2/15/91	1	19.2	7/05/91	98	23.4	11/04/91	34	24.7
2/19/91	2	23.9	7/09/91	54	23.1	11/05/91	22	25.5
2/20/91	3	24.2	7/16/91	217	22.5	11/06/91	37	24.8
2/22/91	1	23.9	7/17/91	15	23.0	11/13/91	18	23.7
2/24/91	0	25.2	8/20/91	17	24.5	11/14/91	45	24.1
2/25/91	2	22.3	8/21/91	0	23.7	11/15/91	55	23.7
2/27/91	0	23.8	8/22/91	0	23.9	11/20/91	16	23.7
2/28/91	0	23.3	8/31/91	10	24.6	11/21/91	34	22.5
3/19/91	2	21.2	9/01/91	17	23.8	12/03/91	38	23.6
4/11/91	123	23.9	9/02/91	11	23.7	12/18/91	17	23.5
4/28/91	18	19.3	9/03/91	34	24.0			
4/29/91	150	27.5	9/14/91	56	16.7	Totals	5320	2615.9
5/02/91	15	24.3	9/15/91	95	23.4			
5/07/91	62	21.3	9/16/91	120	24.7			
5/09/91	78	22.3	9/24/91	21	23.4			
5/10/91	91	20.8	9/26/91	19	23.7			
5/11/91	28	20.8	10/01/91	20	24.8			
5/14/91	1	24.2	10/02/91	46	24.7			
5/16/91	182	22.0	10/03/91	102	22.7			
5/17/91	127	20.2	10/04/91	118	21.6			
5/21/91	11	24.3	10/05/91	24	20.2			
5/24/91	20	24.2	10/06/91	64	23.4			
5/25/91	82	21.5	10/07/91	188	23.1			
5/29/91	16	20.7	10/08/91	98	24.4			
5/30/91	54	24.3	10/09/91	15	22.2			
5/31/91	61	24.2	10/10/91	44	24.4			
6/07/91	39	20.3	10/11/91	35	24.0			
6/08/91	69	24.0	10/12/91	32	27.3			
6/09/91	78	23.7	10/13/91	28	23.0			

Johnson et al. (1994) found that increasing the number of days sampled had diminishing value in improving the precision of the entrainment estimate. They also found that the precision of the estimate varied by season and site.

Derr et al. (1993) suggest evaluating the proposed sampling schedule in the POC study if sampling for less than 24 hours is proposed. We found, however, that diel entrainment rates changed between species and sampling months too often to suggest that sampling is not necessary during any part of the day at a specific site (see Section 3.2.1). Data on diel patterns can be obtained during 24-hour sampling because samples are usually regularly removed from the nets to minimize collection stress to fish. If such data indicate a strong diel trend at a specific site, the feasibility of adjusting daily plant operations to minimize entrainment can be evaluated. Such trends, however, were uncommon across species for sites that we evaluated.

4.5.2 Guidelines for Hydroacoustic Studies

Fixed-location hydroacoustic techniques can effectively document the number and behavior of fish passing through hydroelectric projects. Extensive data can be collected on both temporal and spatial aspects of entrainment. Behavioral aspects of fish entrainment (such as depth or location of entrainment) can be used to determine the most effective types of protective measures at a specific site. These specific temporal and spatial data are rarely available from netting studies.

The success of entrainment studies that rely on hydroacoustic equipment, however, depends on the proper deployment of systems, collection of data, and data analysis. The equipment must be state-of-the-art and operated by properly trained personnel (HTI, 1993). We recommend professional training for all individuals that operate hydroacoustic equipment, review hydroacoustic study plans, and/or interpret the results of hydroacoustic surveys. EPRI (1992b) presents a summary of hydroacoustic methods. In the following section we describe variables that must be included when documenting hydroacoustic studies.

The areal coverage of hydroacoustic transducers is a function of the effective beam width, which is determined by the acoustic size of the target and the distance from the transducer (HTI, 1993). Studies should document the effective beam widths for different target strengths and ranges.

Near- and far-field ensonified zones must be clearly defined during the POC study. The minimum area of the intake to be ensonified should be based on what can be sampled effectively at a specific site and the cost versus sampling bias of a given ensonified field.

The optimal position for transducer placement is as close to the turbines as possible while preventing turbine "noise" from affecting data interpretation. This reduces the likelihood that fish entering the ensonified field that are not entrained will be counted. Water velocity of the ensonified field is typically either measured or calculated based on intake dimensions and turbine hydraulic capacity for each transducer.

USFWS et al. (1992) recommend operating each transducer for a period of no less than 30 minutes every hour and monitoring 24 hours a day for a least 1 year. Although studies in the database do not give the costs, such a sampling regime is conservative and allows licensees/applicants to minimize their initial costs by evaluating some of the data later. The major cost element associated with hydroacoustic studies is data analysis and reporting. If diel entrainment patterns are not part of project objectives, sampling frequency sometimes can be reduced. Site-specific hydroacoustic sampling frequencies may be agreed to during agency consultations.

Most hydroacoustic studies in the database sampled 24 hours each day. At Station 26, sampling was done virtually year-round except when the units were off-line. At Tower, Kleber, and Moores Park, sampling was done 5 days a week during specific periods (every other week or seasonally).

Generally, single-beam transducers with tracking can be used to estimate entrainment rates because they are less sensitive to noise and enable clearer definition of the ensonified area; however, at least one dual beam or split beam transducer per site would enable development of a target strength distribution (convertible to fish length distribution) and effective beam width (convertible to direction of travel), if this measure is needed (HTI, 1993; USFWS et al., 1992).

Before beginning a study, hydroacoustic instrument specifications and proposed operational characteristics should be agreed upon. Systems normally include accurate time varied gain capabilities. During planning, the pulse length, pulse repetition rate (generally no less than 10 "pings" per second), echo signal processor sampling rate, and echo-sounder frequency should be established. Hydroacoustic equipment should be calibrated in accordance with manufacturers' recommendations and protocols agreed upon during consultations. Transducer calibration and overall gain measurement typically require the equipment to be returned to the manufacturer or a qualified acoustic laboratory (HTI, 1993). Documentation of the calibration process along with calibration sheets should be included in the study report, in a pre-approved format. Examples of calibration information developed during previous studies can be used for mutual concurrence or proposed modifications during study planning.

Site-specific noise levels in each turbine bay should be measured during the POC study and transducers placed to optimize detection of the smallest fish included in the study (USFWS et al., 1992). Target-tracking procedures that are proposed to distinguish fish from noise or debris, including the use of filters, should be agreed upon before the entrainment study (USFWS et al., 1992). If noise at a specific site makes detection of small fish uncertain, length-frequency distribution data from net sampling (as done for studies in South Carolina) may be acceptable.

Proposed data extrapolation procedures are less likely to be misunderstood if explained in the study plan. Proposed statistical techniques agreed to by the appropriate agencies also are typically clearly defined in the plan.

Hydroacoustic sampling nearly always is best accompanied by net sampling to determine the species composition and length-frequency distribution of entrained fish. Exceptions to this are rare and require acceptance of assumptions (e.g., that nearly all fish detected are of a certain species or that taxa entrained are similar to that at other facilities where net sampling was conducted) that are best agreed to by the fish and wildlife agencies. If the licensee/applicant cannot agree on this or other study design elements, the FERC resolution process can be used to finalize the study design.

Net sampling also helps to verify the hydroacoustically derived entrainment rate estimates. Net verification was effective at some sites in the database (e.g., Tower, Kleber, and several of the Duke Power sites) but not at others. Estimates that cannot be verified are usually attributed to sampling biases in either the hydroacoustic or netting component of the study. Verification netting typically is used at unit(s) that are hydroacoustically sampled with net sample duration generally corresponding as closely as possible to the actual time that transducers are sampling that unit.

If hydroacoustic entrainment rate estimates vary substantially from net-derived entrainment rate estimates, one of the two techniques probably is providing false values. Equipment should be checked and repairs and adjustments made as appropriate. Some differences between the two techniques, however, are expected in all cases. It is unlikely that intrusion and extrusion can be completely eliminated from net sampling, and it is rarely possible to ensonify 100 percent of a turbine intake, so hydroacoustic counts must be extrapolated to unsampled areas. During study design, the agencies and the licensee/applicant should agree on the limits of variability and what will be done if the results exceed these limits. Hydroacoustic entrainment rate estimates can be compared regularly with netting data (e.g., on a monthly basis) to identify corrective action before the study is completed.

As discussed above, hydroacoustic monitoring techniques are almost always used in conjunction with netting techniques. It may, therefore, be more appropriate to use hydroacoustics to supplement netting studies, rather than the converse. This approach, which was used at Crowley, combines attributes of both methods. At Crowley, hydroacoustics were used to monitor the number of fish entrained at both units. The number of fish of each species that were entrained at the unit not sampled was estimated as follows:

$$\text{ENTRAIN}_{\text{Unit A}} = \text{NETCOUNT}_{\text{Unit B}} \times (\text{HACOUNT}_{\text{Unit A}}/\text{HACOUNT}_{\text{Unit B}})$$

where:

$\text{ENTRAIN}_{\text{Unit A}} =$ the number of a particular species entrained at the unit not sampled by nets;

$\text{NETCOUNT}_{\text{Unit B}} =$ the number of a particular species entrained at the unit sampled by nets;

$\text{HACOUNT}_{\text{Unit A}} =$ the total number of fish entrained at unit not sampled by nets as determined by hydroacoustics; and

$\text{HACOUNT}_{\text{Unit B}} =$ the total number of fish entrained at unit sampled by nets as determined by hydroacoustics.

We suggest calculating the ratio $\text{HACOUNT}_{\text{Unit A}}/\text{HACOUNT}_{\text{Unit B}}$ at least monthly to minimize bias because entrainment patterns are likely to change over time. This method assumes that species composition at the unit not sampled by nets is similar to the unit sampled by nets. It avoids the assumption, however, that the entrainment rate at an unsampled unit is similar to that at a sampled unit.

4.5.3 Guidelines for Reporting Entrainment Study Results

Entrainment studies estimate the number of fish entrained through a hydropower project during a specified time period. Usually this period is 1 year, but it could be less if the plant does not operate continuously (e.g., the plant shuts down for routine maintenance for 1 month). We recommend monthly reporting of entrainment rates (fish/hour) and flows through sampled units. Assumptions used to account for unsampled periods should be clearly stated.

Data from some studies (i.e., without penstocks or power canals) indicate that the entrainment rate may not be uniform at different hydroplant units. We recommend reporting the entrainment rate at different sampled units (both monthly and annual rates) in addition to the annual entrainment rate at the entire project, where applicable. Future assessments then can consider unit-specific protective measures. For example, if a unit routinely does not operate during periods of high entrainment, protective measures may not be needed. If a unit consistently has higher entrainment rates than other units operating during the same time, the sequence of turbine operation may be modified to minimize entrainment during critical periods.

We recommend reporting annual entrainment rates by size interval for each species. Because there is little standardization in reporting size of entrained fish, it is difficult to compare specific-sized fish among sites. We suggest adopting the length intervals associated with the replacement values of fish derived by the American Fisheries Society in the most recent version of "Investigation and Valuation of Fish Kills" (American Fisheries Society, 1991) as the reporting standard. Generally, fish would be reported in 1-inch size intervals, but size intervals could be lumped for certain species, such as clupeids. It would not be necessary to measure the length of certain small species (e.g., most species of minnows).

If this size reporting convention is used, the resource value of entrained fish can be estimated. Affected resources then can be compared among sites. Eventually, criteria may be established for determining the appropriateness of protective measures to minimize entrainment rates based on affected resource values. There is no universally accepted method to determine the value of a fish (Francfort et al., 1994), and few entrainment studies report entrainment rates in a manner that would allow comparable resource value determinations.

Recent turbine mortality studies show that the number of entrained fish that are killed is often relatively small, especially for small fish; for many species numbers are as low as 1 to 3 percent (EPRI, 1992b). If turbine mortality is studied along with entrainment, then the value of the lost resource can be estimated. The significance of these entrainment losses to the fish community in the impoundment, however, is not readily characterized (see Section 4.3).

We recommend reporting the following environmental variables at least daily (agencies may recommend more frequent recording) during sample collection:

- total river discharge (cfs);

- discharge through each unit, including those not sampled (cfs);

- surface, mid-, and bottom forebay temperature and dissolved oxygen; and

- water transparency (Secchi disk value).

We also recommend recording the amount of time sampled during each day and clearly explaining and documenting any deviations from the agreed-upon sampling protocol. Summary tables of these variables should be included in the main body of the report; place the raw data as an appendix. We further recommend reporting the angle of the trashracks relative to the flow into the unit and logging weather conditions during sampling to be used for explanatory purposes, as needed.

We recommend developing and reporting a vertical and horizontal velocity profile of the plant unit being sampled. The intervals at which measurements are recorded depend on site-specific characteristics, and the profile should be based on measurements taken directly upstream of the trashracks. Data should clearly specify whether the profile is oriented perpendicular to the water surface or parallel to the plane of the trashracks. Measurements should be taken during low, average, and high through-plant discharges. We also recommend using average velocity values derived from calculations using forebay dimensions only to generally indicate approach velocity when actual measurements are not available or practical. The average velocity in the collection nets also can be directly measured and reported if anything other than full-flow tailrace netting is used. For studies using hydroacoustics, velocity profiles also can be developed for the ensonified fields using direct measurements or calculated values.

The study report should describe all statistical tests used for data analysis, along with significance levels and confidence intervals and assumptions. All calibration data for hydroacoustic equipment can be included as an appendix.

Quarterly progress reports also should be submitted to appropriate agencies. The frequency of these reports should be established during pre-study consultations. If there are potential deviations from the study plan (e.g., net collection efficiency decreases or forebay noise level changes that would warrant changing the transducer locations in a hydroacoustic study), we recommend contacting the appropriate agencies as soon as possible. Feedback on study results and any deviations from the study plan then can be considered when planning subsequent sampling efforts, rather than after the original sampling effort is completed. The feedback should focus on study plan interpretation and should not add new study components unless agreed upon by both agencies and the licensee/applicant.

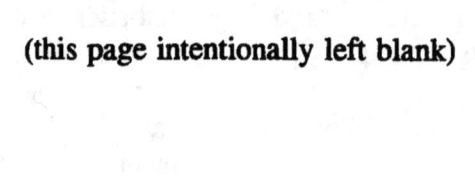

(this page intentionally left blank)

5.0 CONCLUSIONS

As the 45 studies in the database demonstrate, entrainment study design and implementation vary greatly. Variability is a function of the parties conducting the studies, site-specific constraints, costs of conducting the studies, differing resource agency objectives, and the presence or absence of precedents and other guidance. Entrainment study results also show diel, seasonal, spatial, site-specific, and species-specific trends. Overall, we were unable to detect many consistent statistically significant trends, using entrainment rates for all species and sizes combined based on the variables analyzed.

Variability attributable to differences in sampling methods cannot be separated from actual differences in entrainment rates. Our review of these differences leads us to the most important conclusion of this study: Study methods and implementation must be standardized as much as possible. This report presents guidelines to use as building blocks for a standard sampling protocol. Standardization of sampling is an iterative process also, one that requires sharing lessons learned from past experience and adjusting them as new data are gathered. Because of the evolving nature of entrainment sampling methods and impact assessment, this report should not be interpreted by the reader as a FERC policy document.

Presently, extrapolation of total entrainment rates from sampled sites to unsampled sites may be appropriate in some basins. This is especially supportable if evaluation of the need for protective measures can be based on entrainment rates that could be somewhat higher or lower than the actual rate at unsampled sites. Lumping of sampled sites to exclude sites that are not comparable to unsampled sites may reduce potential bias. For example, if the fish community in a reservoir is strongly dominated by clupeids or an upstream stocking program, that site may not be very comparable to other sites without these characteristics. Additional analysis may help eliminate other sites from those considered for lumping and extrapolation. Site-specific entrainment studies may yield more precision at sites with dissimilar site characteristics or species composition. However, the cost of the studies and the expected level of impact would influence the decision of whether or not to conduct such studies.

The cost of conducting entrainment studies is high, but the cost of installing protective measures to minimize entrainment rates is generally higher. Deciding whether or not site-specific entrainment studies are recommended and when study results indicate that protective measures are necessary may affect a project's economic viability.

The results of new entrainment studies could be added to this database or a new database developed to incorporate standardized fish-length data by species. The latter could reduce some of the inter-site variability found in our present analysis. Increasing the amount of available data would improve the statistical reliability of subsequent analyses. Proposed standardized entrainment study protocols can be continually updated and made readily available to agencies, licensees/applicants, and consultants. The Entrainment Review Team also may act as a forum to evaluate proposed future modifications to entrainment sampling and analysis protocols.

Because each site is unique, FERC staff will continue to assess entrainment impacts on a case-by-case basis. If the impact on resources at a site is expected to be high, accurate entrainment estimates will strengthen the basis for determining if fish protection is required. In such cases, realistic conceptual cost estimates for site-specific protective measures may provide a basis to forgo entrainment studies. If anticipated impacts are low relative to the costs of entrainment studies or protective measures, then neither studies nor protective measures may be required.

6.0 LITERATURE CITED

6.1 Literature Cited in the Interpretive Report

American Fisheries Society. 1991. Investigation and Valuation of fish kills. American Fisheries Society Special Publication 24.

Anderson, J.J. 1988. Diverting Migrating Fish Past Turbines. Northeast Environmental Journal 4: 109-128. (as cited by Kynard 1993).

Clark, D.E. 1981. The Wedgewire Screen: A Part of the Sullivan Plant Downstream Migrant Bypass System. Manuscript. Portland General Electric Company. Portland, Oregon.

Clark, D.E. and D.P. Cramer. 1993. Evaluation of the Downstream Migrant Bypass System - T.W. Sullivan Plant, Willamette Falls. Portland General Electric Company. Portland, Oregon.

Consumers Power Company (CPC). 1985. 1985 Report of Deterrent Net Performance, J.R. Whiting Plant. Presented to the Michigan Water Resources Commission.

CPC and the Detroit Edison Company. 1992. Ludington Pumped Storage Project; 1990 Annual Report of Barrier Net Operation. Submitted to FERC December 29, 1992.

Derr, J.A., H.E. Zich, R.F. Carline, and L.M. Young. 1993. Sampling Protocol for Estimating Entrainment and Turbine Mortality of Fish at Hydropower Sites. Prepared by PA State Univ. Statistical Consulting Center for USFWS. Coop. Agreement No. 14-16-0009-1548 Work Order: 41.

Energy & Environmental Management, Inc. 1992. Millville Hydro Station. FERC Project No. 2343. License Articles 405 & 406. 1991 Fish Entrainment Studies and Economic Worth of Lost Fishery. Prepared for the Potomac Edison Company and the Allegheny Power Service Corporation West Virginia.

Environmental Resource Associates, Inc. 1984. Lake Erie Barrier Net, A Feasibility Study. Technical Report 61 Report to Cleveland Electric Illuminating Co.

Electric Power Research Institute (EPRI). 1986. Assessment of Downstream Migrant Fish Protection Technologies for Hydroelectric Application. Prepared by Stone & Webster Engineering Corporation. EPRI Report 2694-1.

EPRI. 1992a. Evaluation of the Eicher Screen at Elwha Dam: 1990 and 1991 Test Results. Prepared by Stone & Webster Engineering Corporation. EPRI TR-101704.

EPRI. 1992b. Fish Entrainment and Turbine Mortality Review and Guidelines. Prepared by Stone & Webster Engineering Corporation. EPRI TR-101231.

EPRI. 1992c. Evaluation of Strobe Lights for Fish Diversion at the York Haven Hydroelectric Project. Prepared by Stone & Webster Engineering Corporation. EPRI TR-101703.

EPRI. 1994a. Biological Evaluation of a Modular Inclined Screen for Diverting Fish at Water Intakes. Prepared by Stone & Webster Engineering Corporation. EPRI TR-104121.

EPRI. 1994b. Research Update on Fish Protection Technologies for Water Intakes. Prepared by Stone & Webster Engineering Corporation. EPRI TR-104122.

Eugene Water and Electric Board (EWEB). 1993. Design information and test data from the Leaburg screening facility. Transmitted to Stone & Webster Engineering Corporation.

Francfort, J.E., G.F. Cada, D.D. Dauble, R.T. Hunt, D.W. Jones, B.N. Rinehart, G.L. Sommers, and R.J. Costello. 1994. Environmental Mitigation at Hydroelectric Projects. Vol. II. Benefits and Costs of Fish Passage and Protection. Prepared for the U.S. Dept. of Energy.

Georgia Pacific Corporation. 1988. Downstream Passage of Atlantic Salmon Smolts and Kelts at Weldon Dam. Mattaceunk Project FERC No. 2520.

Harza Engineering Company and RMC Environmental Services. 1992. Response of Atlantic Salmon Smolts to Louvers in the Holyoke Canal, Spring 1992. Prepared for Northeast Utilities Service Company Berlin, Connecticut.

Harza Engineering Company and RMC Environmental Services. 1993. Response of Juvenile Clupeids to Louvers in the Holyoke Canal, Fall 1992. Prepared for Northeast Utilities Service Company Berlin, Connecticut.

Hosey and Associates and Fish Management Consultants. 1990. Evaluation of the Chandler, Columbia, Roza, and Easton Screening Facilities. Completion Report for the Bureau of Reclamation Yakima, Washington.

Hydroacoustic Technology, Inc.(HTI). 1993. Using Hydroacoustics for Fisheries Assessments. Manual for 2-day short course.

Johnson, G.E., J.R. Skalski, and D.J. Degan. 1994. Statistical precision of hydroacoustic sampling of fish entrainment at hydroelectric facilities. North American Journal of Fisheries Management. 14:323-333.

Klinect, D.A., P.H. Loeffelman, and J.H. Van Hassel. 1992. A New Signal Development Process and Sound System for Diverting Fish from Water Intakes. American Power Conference. pp. 427-432.

Kynard, G. 1993. Anadromous Fish Behavior Important for Fish Passage. In: Proceedings of the Workshop on Fish Passage at Hydroelectric Developments. (Eds.) U.P. Williams, D.A. Scruton, R.F. Goosney, C.F. Bourgeois, D.C. Orr, and C.P. Ruggles. Canada Technical Report of Fish and Agricultural Sciences, No. 1905. pp. 95-105.

Lawler, Matusky & Skelly Engineers (LMS). 1986. Research Coordination for Field Testing of Cooling Water Intake System. 1985 Annual Report to Electric Power Research Institute Research Project 2214-4.

Loeffelman, P.H., D.A. Klinect, J.H. Van Hassel. 1991. Fish Protection at Water Intakes Using a New Signal Development Process and Sound System. Waterpower '91. pp. 354-365.

Neitzel, D.A., T.J. Clune, and C.S. Abernethy. 1990. Evaluation of Rotary Drum Screens Used to Project Juvenile Salmonids in the Yakima River Basin. In: Proceedings of the International Symposium on Fishways '90. Gifu, Japan.

Nettles, D.C., and S.P. Gloss. 1987. Migration of Landlocked Atlantic Salmon Smolts and Effectiveness of a Fish Bypass Structure at a Small-Scale Hydroelectric Facility. North American Journal of Fisheries Management. Vol. 7:562-568.

Northeast Utilities Service Company (NUSCO). 1993. Annual Report on Anadromous Fish Passage Activities and Facilities; Merrimack River, Eastman Falls and Ayers Island Projects. Letter report to Lois Cashell, Federal Energy Regulatory Commission, dated February 26, 1993.

Public Service Company of New Hampshire (PSNH). 1992. Downstream Migration of Atlantic Salmon Smolts at PSNH Hydroelectric Stations on the Merrimack and Pemigewasset Rivers 1989-1990. Final Project Report.

Raemhild, G., B. Ransom, B. Ross, and M. Dimmitt. 1984. Hydroacoustic Assessment of Downstream Migrating Salmon and Steelhead at Rock Island Dam in 1983. Report to Chelan Co. PUD No. 1 Wenatchee, Washington.

Ross, Q.E., D.J. Dunning, R. Thorne, J.K. Menezes, G.W. Tiller, and J.K. Watson. In Press. Response of Alewives to High Frequency Sound at a Power Plant Intake on Lake Ontario. Submitted to North American Journal of Fisheries Management.

RMC Environmental Services, Incorporated. 1993. Evaluation of Mitigative Measures for Juvenile Blueback Herring at the Little Falls Hydroelectric Project. Prepared for Little Falls Hydroelectric Associates.

Sale, M.J., G.F. Cada, L.H. Chang, S.W. Christensen, S.F. Railsback, J.E. Francfort, B.N.
   Rinehart, and G.L. Sommers. 1991. Environmental Mitigation at Hydroelectric Projects Vol. I. Current Practices for Instream Flow Needs, Dissolved Oxygen, and Fish Passage. Prepared for the U.S. Dept. of Energy.

SAS. 1989. JMP Users Guide, Version 2 of JMP. SAS Institute Inc. Cary North Carolina.

Smith, H. 1993. Puntledge Hydro Fish Screens: Eicher Screen. Presented at the 1993 American Fisheries Society Symposium on Fish Passage Responsibility and Technology, September 1-2, 1993, Portland, Oregon.

Stone & Webster Engineering Corporation. 1991. Evaluation of a Barrier Net for Preventing Turbine Passage at the Pine Hydroelectric Project. Prepared for Wisconsin Electric Power Company.

Taft, E.P., S. A. Amaral, F. C. Winchell, and C.W. Sullivan. In Press. Biological Evaluation of a New Modular Fish Diversion Screen. To be presented and published in the AFS Bioengineering Symposium, September 1993.

Thorne, R.E. 1992. Acoustic Estimation of Fish Entrainment, Analysis of Sources of Error - With Special Reference to Wisconsin Entrainment Projects. Prepared for State of Wisconsin Department of Natural Resources by BioSonics, Inc. March 27, 1992.

U.S. Fish and Wildlife Service (USFWS), Wisconsin Department of Natural Resources, and Michigan Department of Natural Resources. 1992. Joint Agency Fish Entrainment/Turbine Mortality Study Plan Guidelines. Vol. 2: Entrainment and Turbine Mortality Studies, Appendix III: Fish Entrainment and Turbine Mortality Study Plan Guidelines.

Vogel, D.A., K.R. Marine and J.G. Smith. 1990. A Summary of Upstream and Downstream Anadromous Salmonid Passage at Red Bluff Diversion Dam on the Sacramento River, California, U.S.A. In: Proceedings of the International Symposium on Fishways '90. Gifu, Japan.

Weyerhaeuser Paper Co.(Weyerhaeuser), Consolidated Water Power Co., and Nekoosa Papers, Inc. 1993. Assessment of Effects of Entrainment and Turbine Mortality on Fish Populations at Selected Hydroelectric Projects on the Wisconsin River.

Winchell, F., S. Amaral, N. Taft, and C. Sullivan. 1993. Biological Evaluation of a Modular Fish Screen. Waterpower '93.

6.2 Entrainment Study Reports Included in the Database

Barnes Williams Environmental Consultants, Inc. (BWEC). 1993. Fish Entrainment Monitoring Program. Lower Hydroelectric Project Flambeau River, Price County, Wisconsin. FERC Project No. 2421-004. Prepared for the Flambeau Paper Corporation, Park Falls, Wisconsin.

BWECo. 1993. Fish Entrainment Monitoring Program Upper. Hydroelectric Station Flambeau River, Price County, Wisconsin. FERC Project No. 2640-011. Prepared for the Flambeau Paper Corporation, Park Falls, Wisconsin.

BWECo. 1993. Fish Entrainment Monitoring Program. Pixley Hydroelectric Project Flambeau River, Price County, Wisconsin. FERC Project No. 2395-004. Prepared for the Flambeau Paper Corporation, Park Falls, Wisconsin.

Barnes Williams Environmental Services. 1993. Fish Entrainment Monitoring Program. Crowley Hydroelectric Station, Flambeau River, Price County, Wisconsin. FERC Project No. 2473. Prepared for the Flambeau Paper Corporation, Park Falls, Wisconsin.

Barnes Williams Environmental Services. 1992. Fish Entrainment Monitoring Program. Balsam Row Hydroelectric Station, Shawano, Wisconsin. Prepared for Mead and Hunt Consulting Engineers, Madison, Wisconsin, on behalf of Wisconsin Power & Light Co.

Barnes Williams Environmental Consultants, Inc. 1991. Fish Entrainment Monitoring Program. Lock and Dam 2 Hydroelectric Project. FERC Project No. 4306-008. Prepared for the City of Hastings, Minnesota.

BioSonics, Inc., and Beak Consultants, Inc. 1991. Fish Entrainment Studies Using Hydroacoustics at Station 26 on the Genesee River. Prepared for Rochester Gas and Electric Corporation Rochester, New York.

Bohr, J. 1990. Fish Entrainment and Mortality Studies at the French Landing Hydroelectric Project on the Huron River, Michigan. Prepared for STS Hydropower, Ltd. Lansing, Michigan.

CH^{2}M HILL and BioSonics. 1988. Fish Population and Entrainment Studies for the Vanceburg Hydroelectric Generating Station No. 1. Prepared for the City of Vanceburg, Kentucky.

Dames and Moore (D&M). 1992. Final Report, Fish Entrainment Studies, Weyerhaueser Company, Rothschild Hydroelectric Project. Prepared for the Weyerhaeuser Company Rothschild, Wisconsin.

Duke Power. 1991. Excerpt from the Saluda application for license to the FERC Provided by Duke Power to Stone & Webster Engineering Corporation.

Duke Power. 1991. Excerpt from the Hollidays Bridge application for license to the FERC Provided by Duke Power to Stone & Webster Engineering Corporation.

Duke Power. 1991. Excerpt from the Gaston Shoals application for license to the FERC Provided by Duke Power to Stone & Webster Engineering Corporation.

Duke Power. 1991. Excerpt from the Ninety-Nine Islands application for license to the FERC Provided by Duke Power to Stone & Webster Engineering Corporation.

Duke Power Company (Duke Power). 1992. Buzzard's Roost Hydroelectric Station. Response to Schedule B, Question 7, Fish Entrainment and Entrainment Mortality at Buzzard's Roost Hydroelectric Project, South Carolina. Duke Power Company, Charlotte, North Carolina.

EA Engineering, Science, and Technology (EA). 1991. Studies of Fish Entrainment and St. Joseph River Fish Populations Near the Constantine Hydroelectric Project. FERC Project 10661. Prepared for Michigan Power Company, Indiana Michigan Power Company and American Electric Power Columbus, Ohio.

EA. 1991. Studies of Fish Entrainment, Smolt Migration, and St. Joseph River Fish Populations Near The Buchanan Hydroelectric Project. FERC Project 2551. Prepared for the Indiana Michigan Power Company and American Electric Power Environmental and Technical Assessment Division Columbus, Ohio.

Energy & Environmental Management, Inc. (EEM). 1993. Letter from John B. Cliff III, dated May 6, to Doug Hjorth (Stone & Webster) providing updated entrainment information for the Millville and Dam 4 projects.

EEM. 1992. Millville Hydro Station. FERC Project No. 2343. License Articles 405 & 406. 1991 Fish Entrainment Studies and Economic Worth of Lost Fishery. Prepared for the Potomac Edison Company and the Allegheny Power Service Corporation West Virginia.

EEM. 1991. Millville Hydro Station. FERC Project No. 2343. License Articles 405 & 406. 1990 Fish Entrainment Studies and Economic Worth of Lost Fishery. Prepared for the Potomac Edison Company and the Allegheny Power Service Corporation West Virginia.

EEM. 1990. Millville Hydro Station. FERC Project No. 2343. License Articles 405 & 406. 1989 Fish Entrainment Studies and 1988 & 1989 Economic Worth of Lost Fishery. Prepared for the Potomac Edison Company and the Allegheny Power Service Corporation West Virginia.

EEM. 1986. Dam No. 4 Hydro Station. Installation of Unit No. 3 1985 and 1986 Field Studies Report. Prepared for the Potomac Edison Company and the Allegheny Power Service Corporation West Virginia.

Harza. 1993. Final Report on Fish Entrainment Studies at the Wisconsin River Division Hydroelectric Project. FERC Project No. 2590. Prepared for Consolidated Water Power Co. Wisconsin Rapids, Wisconsin.

Harza. 1992. Park Mill Hydroelectric Station, (FERC No. 2744). Article 401 Fish Entrainment Study, April 1990-March 1991. Prepared for Scott Worldwide, Scott Paper Company Marinette, Wisconsin.

Harza Engineering Company. 1992. Final Report on Fish Entrainment Studies at the Centralia Hydroelectric Project, FERC Project No. 2255. Prepared for BVMCA, Kansas City, MO and Nekoosa Papers Inc. Port Edwards, Wisconsin.

Harza Engineering Company (Harza). 1991. Evaluation of Entrainment of Fish Through Turbines at Dam 1 and Dam 3. Prepared for the Mead Corporation, Escanaba River Hydroelectric Project Escanaba, Michigan.

Hydroacoustic Technology, Inc. (HTI). 1992. Hydroacoustic and Netting Evaluations of Fish Entrainment and Mortality at Moores Park Dam during 1990 and 1991. Prepared for Lansing Board of Water and Light Lansing, Michigan.

Hydroacoustic Technology, Inc. 1991. Hydroacoustic Evaluation of Fish Entrainment at Tower and Kleber Dams, Final Report. Prepared for Wolverine Power Supply Cooperative Cadillac, Michigan.

Kleinschmidt Associates (KS). 1992. Fish Entrainment Study, Final Report. Prepared for Beaver Falls Municipal Authority Beaver Falls, Pennsylvania.

Kleinschmidt Associates, 1990. Final Report, Fish Entrainment Study. Prepared for Elkem Metals Company Pittsburgh, Pennsylvania.

Lawler Matusky & Skelly Engineer (LMS). 1991. Fish Entrainment Monitoring Program Alcona Hydroelectric Project. Prepared for the Consumers Powers Company Jackson, Michigan.

LMS. 1991. Fish Entrainment Monitoring Program Five Channels Hydroelectric Project. Prepared for the Consumers Powers Company Jackson, Michigan.

LMS. 1991. Fish Entrainment Monitoring Program Mio Hydroelectric Project. Prepared for the Consumers Powers Company Jackson, Michigan.

LMS. 1991. Fish Entrainment Monitoring Program Loud Hydroelectric Project. Prepared for the Consumers Powers Company Jackson, Michigan.

LMS. 1991. Fish Entrainment Monitoring Program Cooke Hydroelectric Project. Prepared for the Consumers Powers Company Jackson, Michigan.

LMS. 1991. Fish Entrainment Monitoring Program Foote Hydroelectric Project. Prepared for the Consumers Powers Company Jackson, Michigan.

LMS. 1991. Fish Entrainment Monitoring Program Croton Hydroelectric Project. Prepared for the Consumers Powers Company Jackson, Michigan.

LMS. 1991. Fish Entrainment Monitoring Program Hardy Hydroelectric Project. Prepared for the Consumers Powers Company Jackson, Michigan.

LMS. 1991. Fish Entrainment Monitoring Program Rogers Hydroelectric Project. Prepared for the Consumers Powers Company Jackson, Michigan.

Normandeau Associates, Inc. (NAI). 1992. Final Study Results and Recommendations, Fish Entrainment Study, FERC Project No. 9988-001, Article 401, John P. King Mill Project, Augusta, Georgia. Prepared for Spartan Mills Augusta, Georgia.

RMC Environmental Services, Inc. 1991. Prickett Hydroelectric Project Entrainment and Turbine Mortality Report. Prepared for Stone & Webster Michigan, Inc. Englewood, Colorado.

R. W. Beck and Associates (RWBeck) and Dames & Moore. 1992. Application for Original License, Major Water Power Project Five Megawatts or Less for the Abbeville Hydroelectric Project FERC Docket No. UL 88-31. Prepared for the City of Abbeville, South Carolina.

RMC Environmental Services, Inc. (RMC), and BioSonics, Inc. 1992. Final Report, Entrainment Studies at the Brule Hydroelectric Project, FERC #2431. Summary of Hydroacoustic Studies and Details of the Net Studies. Prepared for the Wisconsin Electric Power Company Milwaukee, Wisconsin.

RMC Environmental Services, Inc. 1992. Final Report, Study Plan to Assess the Impact of Power Plant Operations on Fish Resources, Youghiogheny Hydroelectric Project. Prepared for D/R Hydro Company Monroeville, Pennsylvania.

RMC Environmental Services, Inc. and BioSonics, Inc. 1992. Final Report Entrainment Studies at the White Rapids Hydroelectric Project FERC #2357. Summary of Hydroacoustic Studies and Details of Net System Studies. Prepared for the Wisconsin Electric Power Company Milwaukee, Wisconsin.

U.P. Engineering and Architectural Associates, Inc. (UPE&AA). 1992. Thornapple Hydroelectric Facility, Fish Entrainment and Mortality Study, Final Report. Prepared for Northern States Power Company Eau Claire, Wisconsin.